THE PLAYBOOK
FOR DADS

The Playbook
FOR DADS

*Parenting Your Kids in
the Game of Life*

JIM KELLY

with Ted Kluck

Faith
Words

New York • Boston • Nashville

FaithWords
Hachette Book Group
237 Park Avenue
New York, NY 10017

www.faithwords.com

Printed in the United States of America

RRD-C

First Edition: September 2012
10 9 8 7 6 5 4 3 2 1

FaithWords is a division of Hachette Book Group, Inc.
The FaithWords name and logo are trademarks of Hachette Book Group, Inc.

The Hachette Speakers Bureau provides a wide range of authors for speaking events. To find out more, go to www.hachettespeakersbureau.com or call (866) 376-6591.

The publisher is not responsible for websites (or their content) that are not owned by the publisher.

Library of Congress Cataloging-in-Publication Data

Kelly, Jim, 1960-
The playbook for dads: parenting your kids in the game of life / Jim Kelly with Ted Kluck.—1st ed.
p. cm.
ISBN 978-0-89296-823-7
1. Parenting—Religious aspects—Christianity. 2. Fathers—Religious life. 3. Youth—Religious life. I. Kluck, Ted. II. Title.
BV4529.K455 2012
248.8'421—dc23
2011048559

Jim Kelly: *To my son, Hunter: My one and only son, in your silence you have taught me what's most important in life. I am the husband, father, and man I am today because God used your precious life to reveal my weaknesses and His strength. I know now why God chose you to be my little #12. Together God has allowed us to take part in His great plan through Hunter's Hope; a plan that has changed and continues to change countless lives. I love and miss you more than words can say. I can't wait to see you again and every day is one day closer to that day. I love you little buddy.*

Ted Kluck: *To my sons, Tristan and Maxim. I love you both so much and I'm thankful for the joy that God has given me, through you. I'm also glad you like football.*

Contents

Foreword by Dan Marino   *ix*

Pregame Update: So What Else Is Going On, and
    Why a Book for Dads?   1

LESSON 1: Thankfulness: Grab a Leaf   11

LESSON 2: Confidence: Where Would You Rather
    Be Than Right Here, Right Now?   23

LESSON 3: Respect: Earned and Given   41

LESSON 4: Preparation: Keep Slingin' It, Twelve   63

LESSON 5: Passion: Live Like You Were Dying   75

LESSON 6: Perseverance: When It's Too Tough for
    Them, It's Just Right for Us   99

LESSON 7: Character: You Are Who You Hang With   111

LESSON 8: Responsibility: It Is What It Is
    (But Not Really)   129

LESSON 9: Teamwork: What Is a Hero?   141

LESSON 10: Spiritual Life: A Hope and a Future   169

Postgame Wrap-up   185

Acknowledgments   *187*

Foreword

I have a lot in common with Jim Kelly. We're both Pennsylvania kids, born and raised in a state where football wasn't just a game, but a way of life. We both had tough, blue-collar dads who raised us, for better or worse, with that kind of attitude toward football and life. We both had fathers who worked incredibly hard at unglamorous jobs to give us the opportunities we had. Hard work, toughness, integrity, and competitiveness weren't really options back then; they were the attributes we saw every morning when our dads would wake up while it was still dark to leave the house for work.

You get to know a lot about a person when you compete against them. For years I stood across a field and watched Jim Kelly run his offense, and he watched me run mine. Jim and I both played for high-profile college programs—me at Pitt and him at Miami—and were both a part of the 1983 NFL Draft, which produced some of the most successful and well-known quarterbacks in the history of the league. We both played for pro coaches who let us throw the ball a lot. Our paths crossed quite a bit in those days. As competitors in the old AFC East we played twice a year. There were snowy, cold afternoons in Rich Stadium and hot, humid, rainy afternoons in Miami.

Year after year we would compete like this, and I grew to admire not only who Jim was but the way he played the game.

I saw him play hurt. I saw him deal with controversy in the media. I saw him experience both the elation of going to the Super Bowl (something I was only able to do once) four times and the heartbreak of losing. We share that heartbreak. In a sense, we grew up together on those fields. We saw each other as young men, in our twenties, picked to lead teams and be the "face" of franchises, and as the years passed we watched each other—again across the field—age, mature, and ultimately retire.

One of the unique things about Jim is that he's one of the few people who can understand the demands of my life, and vice versa. After retirement, Jim and I both navigated the worlds of television commentary, public appearances, and ultimately the Pro Football Hall of Fame. We both know what it's like to be husbands and fathers. And we both know the unique blessings and challenges of life with a special-needs child.

It's one thing to play football against someone and know them that way, but when I saw Jim and Jill persevere through Hunter's illness, I grew to love and respect them in an entirely new way. When our son Michael was diagnosed with autism, it changed life for Claire and me forever. Like Jim, I knew the elation of having a son, but also the heartbreak of knowing that his life is going to be uniquely difficult.

The other thing I have in common with Jim is that we're both far from perfect, and Jim would be the first to tell you that. We've both made mistakes, in football and in life. But Jim is a passionate and committed father—he loves his wife and he loves his kids with the same kind of passion and intensity he brought to the football field. Like Jim himself, this book will be intensely practical and always humble. It's my honor to introduce the book for you, as it's been an honor to compete against and share life with Jim Kelly—quarterback, husband, father, and friend.

—*Dan Marino*

THE PLAYBOOK
FOR DADS

So What Else Is Going On, and Why a Book for Dads?

"So what else is going on?"

That's the phrase that I employ with my wife when I'm done conversing about a particular subject and want to move on, conversationally. It's like page one of the Jim/Jill playbook on interpersonal communication. Subject changing. That's one of what I hope is a variety of new things that you'll learn about me in this book. It occurs to me that athletes usually write memoirs when they're in their midtwenties or early thirties (see *Jim Kelly: Armed and Dangerous*), but most of the interesting stuff that happens to people in their lives happens after that time. That's certainly been the case for me.

This book isn't a memoir, per se. Rather, it's a reflection on some of the things that have happened to me during the years and how I think of those things in light of my most important title: dad. To fans, I'm the guy who used to play quarterback for the Buffalo Bills. Number 12. To my daughters, Cam and Erin, I'm their dad. I'm the guy who helps get them ready for school, occasionally coaches their basketball teams, and tries his best to impart some life lessons. And I've lived a lot of life. I've learned a lot of lessons. Some the hard way.

This book will be lessons and observations bookended by letters—each chapter featuring a letter to my son Hunter at the beginning and a letter to my daughters, Cam and Erin, at the end. In between, each chapter will highlight life lessons that I've learned during my life and career. At the end of each chapter I've included some questions to get you thinking about your own lives and taking the offensive when it comes to teaching these lessons to your own kids.

On paper, at least, I make part of my living showing up to different places and functions and just kind of *being* Jim Kelly. This is not unpleasant, mind you, and people (myself included) seem to enjoy it. It's actually a huge privilege. I spent the last week turkey hunting with actor and country music star Tim McGraw, who is one of the kindest, most genuine people you could ever hope to be around. I'll spend next week playing in a golf tournament hosted by the Shooter McGavin character from the Adam Sandler golf movie *Happy Gilmore*. Shooter, of course, has a real name (Chris McDonald), but his movie character was so iconic that he just goes by Shooter these days. What a hoot he is to be around.

Fame is funny that way. I can drive you down a street in Orchard Park, New York, named Jim Kelly Boulevard, past the Big Tree, a bar in which most of my teammates and I used to bond after Bills practices back in the '80s and '90s. The bar is barely a deep down-and-out away from Ralph Wilson Stadium which is, itself, no more than a handful of down-and-outs away from my house. Surreal. The bar also has a giant likeness of myself, Chris Berman, and Andre Reed in front of it, carved out of wood. I mention this not to brag, but only because it's just, well, surreal. A writer asked me recently if I get recognized around town, and I explained that I think everyone who has ever wanted my autograph in Buffalo has gotten it by now. Buffalo is like a big small town, and I love it for that reason.

Hosting postgame parties at my house was just a small way for me to show my gratitude to my teammates—especially my offensive linemen—guys like Kent Hull, Will Wolford, Howard Ballard, John Davis, Jimmy Ritcher, and others. These were the guys that protected me day in and day out for years and—quite literally—had my back. Expressing gratitude toward the people in your life is one of the themes I hope to explore in this book. It's something that was drilled into me by my parents, and doing it—thanking people—is something that gives me great joy.

The other strange thing about fame is that the kinds of people who may be inclined to read your books already know a litany of things about you. For example, you may well already know that I was planning to attend college at Penn State, but Joe Paterno (the coach of the Nittany Lions then) wanted me to play linebacker. I wanted to play quarterback, so I ended up playing for Howard Schnellenberger at the University of Miami. You may also know that I played the game with a "Linebacker Mentality"—a phrase that is a favorite of sportswriter types and a fancy way of saying that I took a lot of hits (separated shoulders, slipped discs, and more concussions than I can remember—which is why I can't remember) but kept coming back for more. But they don't know how I thought (and think) about those experiences in light of my kids. How I've transferred some of those football and life lessons into the arena of parenting. That's what I hope to accomplish here.

Playing with that linebacker mentality had its drawbacks. Namely the fact that my body is now a road map of pain, and in order to sit comfortably for any length of time (due to a back, neck, and shoulders that were bounced off Astroturf all over the USFL and NFL in the '80s and '90s), I have to prop up the pillows on my living-room sofa just right. And I don't so much sit anymore, but rather kind of *situate*. And the hot tub is my best friend—not in an "MTV Cribs" sort of way, but in a getting my beat-up body through the day sort of way. I just had three metal plates and three screws put into my back.

It also occurs to me that when you make your living playing professional football, even for the healthiest and most blessed among us, your career is over by your midthirties, and then you're looking at several more decades of being you, minus the football. This book, in a sense, is about those decades—what they've looked like up to this point, and what they, Lord willing, will look like in the future. I spent the majority of my life playing the game of my life but living apart from God...but I will finish well—not because of anything I have done but because of all that Christ has done on my behalf. Part of this book will be devoted to telling the stories of what He has done on my behalf—not in a self-righteous, "look at me" sort of way, but in a way that suggests, "Why me?" Why have I been the recipient of such grace? And by grace I don't even mean the money and the fame and the stuff that goes with it. I mean the blessing of a loving, forgiving, devoted wife. The joy I receive from being around my children, and even the grace that came through our darkest hours—losing our son Hunter. And how am I bestowing that grace on my kids? How am I teaching them to avoid some of the mistakes I made along the way?

But here's the thing: this isn't going to be a book full of Christianese about how I started praying and then God made everything perfect. Partly because that isn't true, and partly because I just can't talk like that. I didn't grow up in it, so I don't know how. Christianity wasn't the magic bullet to a perfect life, but it *is* the source of my hope and my identity. The hope that I'll see God, and Hunter, in heaven someday.

When I was a kid growing up in a tight-knit family (note: everybody says this about their families, but it's thankfully entirely true in my case), I had no idea things would turn out like this. I never had the audacity to dream of the NFL Hall of Fame or any of the stuff that comes with it. I dreamed that one day I might play on the Astroturf at Three Rivers Stadium. I pretended to be Terry Bradshaw, like lots of Pennsylvania kids. And I was blessed to be able to play in that stadium as a member of the Buffalo Bills. But the older we get, the more I think we're defined by what we've lost. And I think that the Lord teaches us, and changes us, as much (or more) through what we've lost more than through what we've gained or accomplished.

Speaking of which, let's just get this out of the way now because it's the proverbial elephant in the room: I lost four Super Bowls. I've had the unique experience of reaching this particular professional mountaintop four times in a row, glimpsing how cool and potentially fulfilling it might have been to be the guy on the podium hoisting the Vince Lombardi

Trophy, only to lose each time in a variety of ways—some losses were close (a last-second field goal not going our way), and some were not so close. All are immortalized forever in overproduced NFL Films™ highlight packages which are both a blessing and a curse. A blessing because it was intoxicating to at one point be a young man, running around with the world's greatest athletes, playing the world's greatest game at a pretty high level. A curse because, well, we lost, and losing sucks. But often it is in losing (a game, a job, a loved one) that our character is revealed most clearly. And it is in these losses that our character is developed. I've learned this firsthand.

If you are familiar with my story, you also probably know that Jill and I lost our only son, Hunter, at age eight to a rare illness called Krabbe disease. But very few people knew what it felt like to hold him. What it felt like four months after his birth, when we learned of his condition, to see the father/son dreams of football in the backyard die before my eyes. To ask the "why?" questions of God during a time when I really wasn't talking to God at all. People don't know that for the years Hunter was with us he had to be monitored 24/7...and so we did. Hunter's bravery taught us to be bold. His humility inspired us. His hope encouraged us. And in the midst of that, the day in and day out emotional and physical strain of living with his condition almost destroyed us. Were it not for God's grace.

These are just a few of the things I'll try to communicate in this book. I'll talk about some of the things I dreamed of sharing with Hunter and the lessons I try to share with my girls now.

It's likely that you don't know the dreams I had for raising a boy. Dreams that included sharing with him a lot of the lessons I've learned in football and in life. Those are the things (the lessons) that you don't manage to fit into your Young Athlete Memoir, largely because they haven't been learned yet. Those memoirs are filled with stories about championships and first contracts and teammates and coaches. Those are all good things, but they're not everything and they're definitely not the main thing. There are lessons I dreamed about teaching Hunter, and I'll try to share some of those things with you as well. Everything from how to shake someone's hand and make eye contact when you meet for the first time, to explaining what it feels like to settle in under center, with a few seconds to diagnose a defense, call an audible at the line of scrimmage, ignore the throbbing/searing pain in your shoulder, avoid a pass rush, and then fire a strike downfield (note: this felt amazing).

You may not be aware of the role that my teammates played in my life through all of this. The fact that guys like Steve Tasker and Frank Reich not only battled with me on Sunday afternoons, but battled for me and my family through their prayers and friendship. If football teaches anything, it's that life isn't a game that's played alone. And that's especially true of the Christian life and the family of God. Community, and relationships, happen naturally in football—believe it or not—because a team is united in a common goal, and teammates share the same victories, the same defeats, the same injuries, and the same frustrations.

It was the suffering in my life—losing Hunter and almost losing my marriage to Jill in the process—that ultimately created in me a deep personal change. A peace that surpasses all understanding and a hope that vast amounts of money, success, and fame couldn't come close to bringing. That's the lie that books like these sometimes (intentionally or not) sell you—they sell you on the dream of how fabulous it must be to be (insert name of famous person), but in reality they leave you empty because they don't share anything real.

Books like these tend to sort of be tributes to a famous person, written by that famous person in such a way as to suggest humility, but somehow never really accomplishing it. I don't want to write one of those books. I would rather not write a book at all than write that kind of book.

This is a book about "What Else Is Going On," but it's also a book that isn't going to change the subject on you. The subjects being life, and football, and marriage, and character, and love, and kids, and all of the things that actually matter. The things I would've taught Hunter, had I a lifetime with him to share. And yet, he was the one who actually taught me most of what I'm going to share with you.

In the other room, down the hall from my office, there are a bunch of great guys sitting in a boardroom planning my summer football camp—which has become an annual opportunity for me to share some of these ideas with kids from around the country and hopefully make some kind of an impact on their lives outside of football.

In the corner on the floor, collecting an impressive layer of dust, is my USFL Player of the Year trophy from 1984 when I played with the Houston Gamblers. On the shelves and walls are a ton of pictures of me with other people I respect and call friends—Marv Levy, Dan Marino, Chris Berman, and the guys from Van Halen just to name a few. But as a football player and as a man, if my life is nothing more than the sum of my trips, my trophies, and my pictures with famous people—things on which the world places a great deal of value—then I've failed miserably. And if this book is nothing more than a collection of football and Famous Person stories, then I've failed on that level too.

I'm blessed to be able to sit in this office and write this book. It's an honor, and a little bit of a mindblower to me. But it's an honor and a privilege that I don't take lightly. I'm thankful for the life that the Lord has given me—for the wins *and* the losses, and mostly for the people with whom I'm blessed to be able to share it. I hope you'll be blessed by it too.

Thankfulness: Grab a Leaf

Dear Hunter,

I'm so thankful for the time I had with you. In a way, this book is a collection of all of the things I wish I'd had a chance to teach you and all of the places I wish I could have taken you with me. Although sometimes I think you taught me more in your eight years than I could have ever taught you. But here goes.

Love,
Dad

It's the first day of the twenty-third consecutive year of the Jim Kelly Summer Football Camp for kids. We're indoors at the Buffalo Bills practice facility, and around me are larger-than-life sized photographs of Buffalo Bills legends, current and past. Jack Kemp. Cookie Gilchrist. Joe Ferguson. Bruce Smith. Andre Reed. Steve Tasker. And me. The fact of the matter is that I've been in and out of places like this my entire life... practice fields, stadiums, locker rooms, and indoor facilities. The other fact of the matter is that I still get a kick out of it because I love football.

The field is a swirling mass of humanity. Having done this for twenty-three years, I've gotten pretty good at picking out the cast of characters. There are the cocky high school kids relaxing on the turf...practicing a sort of nonchalance that says "this is no big deal" while on the inside they're eager to impress anyone who will notice them. I know this because I used to be one of them. Then there are the little kids who are just thrilled to be on a football field and don't need to be told to throw a ball or run around, diving on the turf, emulating their heroes. I used to be one of these kids too. I dreamed of playing at Three Rivers Stadium, and when I was a kid in Pennsylvania, I dreamed of being the quarterback, Terry Bradshaw.

And if history is any indicator, some of the kids lolling around on the turf today may be playing here in a few years. A handful of guys who have gone to my camp have ended up in the NFL, including Anthony Dorsett (Tony's kid), Shawn Springs, Marc Bulger, and Jon Corto from the current Bills.

I have a great deal of respect for people's dreams. One of my dreams was to have a son here, as a camper. A few months after Hunter was born, on February 14th (my birthday), 1997, I knew I would never live that dream, and it hurt. I was pissed off at the world for a long time because of that.

Then there are the parents who stand around the edge of the field, trying to keep an eye on their kids while taking it all in. There are the moms with cameras and the dads—some of whom are grown men wearing football jerseys of their favorite heroes (note: I guess some adults never truly grow up, myself included).

In a minute I'll have a megaphone in my hand and be leading stretching and warm-up drills for all five hundred or more campers. I'll try to teach the carioca drill to a group of nine year olds, most of whom will fall down. And, eventually, I'll sign an autograph for every kid at the camp, which, truth be told, is my favorite part of the whole thing. To see the smiles on the kid's faces and the even bigger smiles on their parents' is incredibly humbling and fulfilling. I've always loved throwing a football. I loved it when I was a little kid in the backyard, and I love it now. I'll go to my grave loving it. I'm thankful that I got to make a living doing this.

Somewhere along the sideline is my close friend Greg Zappala who played with me at the University of Miami and used to drive me to class. Zap drove me to class because he always used to say that he "wasn't going to play this game long." I played against Zap in the USFL, when I was with the Houston Gamblers and he was with the Jacksonville Bulls. I played for Mouse Davis (more on him later) in the run-and-shoot offense, where we would pass for about a thousand yards a game and put up video-game numbers. We weren't known for our running game. But when I played against Zap, I came up to the line of scrimmage and he was at middle linebacker, standing about four yards away from me. You have to understand something: football movies have distorted what actually happens at the line of scrimmage. The fact of the matter is that even though you're in a packed stadium (or in the USFL's case, a half-full stadium) and are wearing helmets and shoulder pads, you're still just two people standing there talking to each other. I came up to the line of scrimmage and told Zap, "Hey, stupid, we're going to run it right up the middle, at you, every play this series." I don't think we'd run four times the entire season, but we ran it right at Zap every play and scored on that series. He loves telling that story.

And I'm thankful for my dad, who's here with me today. There's something incredibly satisfying about sharing stuff like this with your dad. Just to be able to look out of the corner of my eye once in a while and watch him watching me. Seeing him brings back so many memories.

He's eighty-two years old and just moved to Buffalo. He's as sharp and independent as ever, and he, more than anybody else, taught me how to work and be tough. Dad wasn't one of these coddling suburban fathers driving his kids to practice in a Lexus, burying his nose in an iPhone and playing politics with the coaches. He had a sixth-grade education and didn't have the benefit of reading books on parenting. He worked in steel mills, worked as a machinist, sold knives door-to-door, and pretty much did whatever he had to do to feed six big, hungry boys. He was laid off sometimes, and a lot of times things were really tough financially. We always shared space. We had four boys to a bedroom at one point, and I remember going to school after Christmas and lying about what I got. I would tell the kids that I got something cool...like Rock 'Em Sock 'Em Robots, but what I really got was a pair of socks.

I can't say enough about my dad. Dad never played a down of organized football, or any other organized sport for that matter. He taught himself all of the sports so that he could in turn teach them to us. His folks died when he was two, and he was raised by nuns at an orphanage near Pittsburgh. My dad spent the majority of his life, even as a kid, working.

I'll never forget him working with me in the backyard, running routes for me. Let me tell you, for a guy who worked all day doing manual labor, Dad still ran a pretty mean route. He had me sprinting out and taking drops and putting the ball on the money. I'll never forget the cold fall air, the cold ball, me out back in a Steelers jersey, and Dad there with me as often as he could be there. After I won a Punt, Pass, & Kick competition as a kid, I got to meet my hero, Terry Bradshaw, and he showed me the "Bradshaw Grip," which involved putting his index finger on the top of the ball and his ring finger on the first lace. "I'm going to take your job one day," I told Bradshaw that day. I've changed the grip style just a little from the first lace to the second, and now I'm the one teaching kids how to do it. Interesting how life works.

When Dad was training me for the Punt, Pass, & Kick competition, he would take our clothesline and stretch it on the ground from one end to the other, marking off the inches and feet. Then, much as the name suggests, I would punt, pass, and kick. Pretty simple. It sounds crazy, but he would make me do a certain number of reps before I could eat lunch! Every day this scene would play out, and some days lunch was forgotten completely. Some days, I won't lie, I didn't want to go home and I didn't want to throw the football. I would avoid him, or curse under my breath, to which he would reply, "What was that, son?" to which I would reply, "Nothing, Dad." And now he's standing on the sidelines at my football camp.

Dad's coaching technique was amazing. He knew that in addition to pointing out the things I did wrong (which he did, believe me), he also knew that when he praised the things I did right, it would mean the world. And it did. When he would yell, "That's my boy!" after I made a good throw, I felt like a million bucks, and I would have run through brick walls for that guy. That's the same way that I try to encourage my two daughters and how I try to reach out to the kids at my camp. Those times with my dad, in the backyard, were as significant to me as the Super Bowls or any of the other experiences I had playing football. The more I'm around, the more I'm convinced that a huge part of this game—a huge part of what makes it satisfying—is who you can share it with.

There are so many football memories that come flooding back at camp. I've got my brothers here, and we all hang out in a big motor home (thanks Chris Colton) that sits right outside the Bills practice facility. Between camp obligations we can all be found in there eating, laughing, catching up on each others' lives, and just enjoying each others' company. When we're not hanging out in the RV, we're zipping around on golf carts, seeing how fast we can go and how tight we can take corners. The great thing about football (and to be candid, sometimes the bad thing about it) is that you can feel like you never have to grow up. Jill jokingly asks me from time to time, "When are you going to grow up?" My response is, "Hopefully never."

All of my brothers would agree that dad's coaching paid off in both big and small ways, for all of us. In 1974 my brother Pat was drafted by the Baltimore Colts, where he spent some time at linebacker. The only time I saw Pat play in person, as a pro, was in 1977 in Canton, Ohio, at the Hall of Fame pre-season game. I was in awe, to say the least. There's something magical about walking up the ramp in a stadium and then walking out and seeing the green grass, the white lines, and all of those players warming up. I'll never forget that day. And to think that my brother was one of them. It blew my mind to see him on the field in an NFL uniform. We went nuts whenever he did anything on the field, as a linebacker or on special teams, and I made sure that everyone sitting around me knew that he was *my* brother. My dad knew how my mind worked, and he knew that it was my dream to be on that field one day, which is why he never let up on me and why he pushed me to work as hard as I could.

My dad loved East Brady, PA, but he knew that it didn't exactly hold a wealth of opportunities for all of his boys. East Brady is located about sixty-five miles northeast of Pittsburgh and features the following: No traffic lights, no department stores, no fast food...but a bunch of bars, a bunch of churches, and a whole lot of great people. East Brady, to put it simply, is the kind of place you love, but the kind of place you ultimately have to leave in search of opportunities.

Dad felt like sports might be our ticket out, and he pushed us accordingly. "Someday you'll thank me for all of this," he said. "If you want something bad enough, you have to work for it. If you work hard for it, chances are you'll receive it. All you have to do is put your mind to it and be patient, and hopefully everything will work out."

We were a tough family, and I think toughness is important. With all of those brothers, there were bound to be fights and disagreements. When my brothers and I fought, Dad would take us into the garage for a little Main Event Therapy. "What's Main Event Therapy?" you ask. It involved boxing gloves, football helmets, and two of us pounding the crap out of each other and then shaking hands at the end, like gentlemen. Dad knew we needed to get the anger and rage out, but he also knew that we needed the bond and we needed to love each other.

With all those boys in a tiny house, we had to be resourceful. We played indoor basketball, and like all cold-weather, football-loving kids, we played knee-football inside, which resulted in countless rug burns, cuts, bruises, and scrapes.

I've kind of been working on this theory that in order to be good at something hard, like football, it has to fill a deep, fundamental need. Football is too hard, otherwise. It doesn't make sense, intuitively, to subject your body to that kind of beating. I've separated shoulders, sprained ankles, and had numerous concussions. It doesn't make sense to do all of that unless you really need it, and I needed football to take care of my parents but also to define myself, early on and even today, truth be told.

A Legacy of Thankfulness

We always took my parents for granted, like most kids do, but when we got older we realized what Mom and Dad went through for us, and a huge motivating force in our lives was the desire to take care of our parents.

My mom's nickname was Saint Alice. She worked in our high school cafeteria to make ends meet, but she always had time to make dinner for her boys and the other neighborhood kids. My mom knew every way imaginable for preparing ground beef and making it into a meal. She got emphysema and suffered for many years before the Lord took her home in 1996. I miss her so much. All of our energy, as brothers, was channeled toward being able to take care of our folks. My mom was also something of a magician in the laundry room. Let me explain. No matter what shape our uniforms were in after games, my mom would work her magic on them and make them look better than new. After a while the other play-ers' moms were on the phone, asking Alice how she got the uniforms so clean! But there was no magic detergent—just a lot of hard work and a lot of pride. Mom scrubbed every last bit of dirt out of those jerseys and pants because she loved us, and even though she couldn't always buy us the newest and the nicest, she always did her best. Those are the kinds of lessons that stay with me, to this day. No matter how much money you have, or how much you've achieved, it's so important to work hard at whatever you're doing, including washing dirty football uniforms.

Dad was tough on us, and he pushed us. Nowadays there are a million books and articles on how to raise athletes and what to do and what not to do. What my dad realized early on is that we had too much free time. We weren't allowed to eat lunch until we'd thrown a certain number of passes.

And whenever I got knocked down on the football field, I could always hear my brothers in the stands yelling for me to "get up." I'm thankful for the toughness that they brought me, which was very visible and public because of the football, but the fact of the matter is that they're all tough in their own way. In rural Pennsylvania, toughness was just a way of life. It wasn't really an option. If you wanted to survive and get along in the world, you had to earn people's respect, and the way you did that was by working hard and getting up off the deck when you got knocked down. It was an old-school way of life, and unfortunately, I feel like it's become the exception today, instead of the norm, like it was back then.

Cultivating Thankfulness

I try to teach the concept of thankfulness here at camp, which is sometimes a challenge, as football players aren't exactly famous for their thoughtfulness and sensitivity. Every year at camp each kid can bring one item through—a jersey, hat, ball, or picture—and get it autographed. As a parent I'm a firm believer in saying "please" and "thank you," and I've tried to instill that in my campers as well. The first several years at camp we jumped on the golf cart and signed autographs for every kid at camp. If a kid would come through the line to get his item signed and wouldn't say "thank you," I'd tell him to go "grab a leaf." Meaning that the kid would have to run a half mile to the tree and back if he didn't say "thanks." I didn't do it because I was obsessed with the "thanks," but rather, because I think it's critically important for kids to be thankful for the privileges they have.

How are you teaching your kids to be thankful? We live in an increasingly thankless culture, and I find that a sincere "thank you" from a young person goes a long way in communicating character. I insist that my girls say "thank you" to clerks, teachers, and especially Mom and Dad. It's a sign of respect and also a way to keep them grounded. I put my parents through a lot of grief, but I think they always knew that I appreciated them. I appreciate them to this day.

Tangibly, make sure your kids are thanking their teachers and their coaches on a regular basis. These folks work hard, often for very little money, and it's easy to take them for granted. A word or a note of thanks goes a long way. And I always make sure my kids write thank-you notes for gifts they've received. It seems like a little thing—and a little old-fashioned, but it goes a long way.

As I stand here, on the field, in the middle of all these kids, with my brothers, Dad, and my close friends hanging out on the sidelines...I'm so thankful. More than I can say. I'm thankful for hard work, for lessons taught and learned, for winning and losing. I'm thankful for moments like this when I can reflect on all that God has done in my life thus far.

Dear Cam and Erin,

I haven't always been as thankful as I should have been—for your mother and for the challenges God put in my life. But I'm so thankful that I get to be your dad. And I'm thankful for the young women you've become. Please take the time to be thankful. We've dealt with so much as a family, but we have so much to be grateful for.

Always,
Dad

OFFENSIVE STRATEGIES

1. In what ways does Jim express thankfulness for his father and brothers?
2. How did Jim's dad cultivate his relationship with his son?
3. How are you expressing and cultivating thankfulness for the people in your life?
4. What are some ways in which you're modeling thankfulness to your kids, even in the midst of trials?
5. How can your kids tangibly thank the people—coaches, teachers, family members—who are key parts of their lives?

Confidence: Where Would You Rather Be Than Right Here, Right Now?

Dear Hunter,

You showed great confidence in your time here on earth. You taught our family so much. So much of my confidence, in retrospect, was false—I was confident in my ability to throw a football, run, and lead my teammates—but you showed me a whole different kind of confidence. The kind that allowed me to trust God with my life and get help when I needed it most. I thank God for that, and I thank Him for you.

Always,
Dad

Where would you rather be than right here, right now? —Marv Levy

I'm writing this from a U.S. military barracks in the Middle East, and there's nowhere I'd rather be than right here, right now. I came over with a group of NFL guys, and we have lived, eaten, and played flag football with the troops who are serving here. It's hot. Everywhere you look there's sand and military equipment. There's a discernable lack of things that I have come to appreciate: namely my bed and my sofa. I have so much respect and admiration for the men and women who put their lives on the line to defend our country and freedoms. What they do takes a tremendous amount of hard work, trust, respect, and confidence.

When you grow up with three older brothers in a small town—and those older brothers are all leaders and successful athletes and captains themselves—you kind of have the run of the place and confidence is a given. It seems like for as long as I can remember I had confidence. As a kid I was always the leader, a captain—on the school yard when it was time to pick teams and in our real leagues. And even off the field, kids would always ask me what we were going to do that day—whether we were going to go swimming, play pickup basketball, or Wiffle ball.

From a young age I had coaches building up my confidence and encouraging me to work hard. I had a coach in youth football named Art Delano who would run up and down the train tracks with me to lose weight and around the football field at least ten times. He taught me the importance of denying myself in the moment so that I could see the hard work pay off down the road.

I'll never forget that when I was ten years old it was the night before our youth football championship game, and I was eating too much—I ate hot dogs, cupcakes, ice cream, and drank a bunch of pop. The next morning we had to weigh in for the game. I was three pounds overweight, couldn't play, and we lost the game. I had to sit on the sidelines in my uniform—all dressed up and nowhere to play.

At that point I learned that the decisions I made impacted others. I felt horrible for letting my team and my family down, and it was the beginning of lifelong lessons in accountability and leadership.

<hr />

As is the case in many small towns, high school football is the biggest (and only) show in town. That was the case in East Brady, home of the Bulldogs. My older brothers had already firmly established the Kelly tradition by the time I got on the field—Pat was a linebacker, Ray played linebacker and quarterback, Ed was a quarterback. My younger brothers continued the tradition—Danny was a wide receiver, and Kevin played offensive line.

Sadly, due to declining enrollments, East Brady High no longer exists. But that just adds to the sort of cinematic quality of the memories. Everything seems like it only exists on Super 8 film. They retired my jersey at East Brady and then turned around and gave it right back to me when the school closed, and now it's sitting in the Pro Football Hall of Fame.

Building Confidence through Success

I became the starting quarterback on varsity as a sophomore, which as you can imagine was quite a lift to my confidence and my sense of belonging in school and in town. I had arrived, in a sense. It was important to me to follow in my brothers' footsteps and make the family proud. There are certain things you never forget about high school football—like wearing the game jersey to school on Fridays and spending that whole day in a fog, just dreaming about the game that was to come. I'll never forget the smell of smoke and popcorn that filled the air above the stadium on Friday nights. Or when we played at home, Saturdays, because we had no lights. And to this day, whenever I hear the sound of drum beats in the distance, I think of high school football.

We were 6-3 in my sophomore year, and I threw fourteen touchdown passes. The following season we were undefeated, and I threw for 1,474 yards and fifteen touchdowns. My senior year we went undefeated again, as I tossed another fifteen scores and left most games at halftime, when we were up by something like 30–0. By the end of my high school career, I had thrown for almost four thousand yards and forty-four touchdowns, helping the Bulldogs to a 25-3-1 record and two Little 12 Conference titles. The Little 12 was made up of a bunch of small schools (enrollment 350 or under) in middle and western Pennsylvania. Another thing I'll never forget is the bus routes to those towns—loading up on a school bus in our uniforms and driving those same routes, over the same back roads to places like Union and Karns City.

I was an all-state selection in high school, and I was also the first Little 12 player in league history to be chosen for the Big 33 State All-Star game. It was heady stuff.

There was one person, in particular, who had as much of an impact on my confidence in life as anyone. Terry Henry, our head coach, was one of those guys who was wise beyond his years. Being that East Brady was a small school, Terry wore many (read: every) hats—he taped ankles before games, he tended to injuries, he taught, he counseled, and he played the role of surrogate father to many of us. There's nothing quite like your high school coach. I think about Terry a lot, and he's a big part of my life to this day.

Terry also kept me grounded and kept my confidence in check. With all the success and accolades that were coming my way, and with the unique experience of being a big fish in a small pond, quite frankly, I was becoming a little bit of a jerk. I hated criticism. I thought I knew better than everybody else (and had a roomful of trophies to prove it), and Terry was there to remind me, along with my brothers, that I wasn't. Thank God I listened to their advice.

He was also good at diffusing conflict. There was a time when Terry took a bunch of us to another town to scout Moniteau High School, a rival of ours. Not surprisingly, some mouthing off took place, and Terry loaded up the van and got us out of there. But a bunch of the Moniteau kids jumped in their cars and chased us. It was like something out of *American Graffiti* or *The Outsiders*. A bunch of cocky high school guys showing off and being dumb. But when Terry decided they weren't going to give up, he slammed on the brakes, and we all piled out of the van and walked right into the middle of the road. A bunch of hyped-up punks. The Moniteau kids were, frankly, freaked out. They did 180s in their cars, and we never saw them again.

Terry Henry is one of my closest friends to this day. I respected the way he hung with me and stuck with me, and now he's a fixture on my hunting and Fellowship of Christian Athletes trips. In fact, recently we were interviewed by the FCA when we were in the middle of a trout stream, with waders on and fishing poles in our hands. One of my lifelong goals was that when I got successful, I would be in a position to take care of the people who were important to me. That included my family, Mom and Dad, my brothers, and Coach Henry.

Building Confidence through Challenge

When Miami head coach Lou Saban flew to Pennsylvania to recruit me, we were in the middle of a blizzard. Saban had to reroute, and the roads to East Brady were covered with snow. Still, when he arrived, he had enough energy to begin cooking dinner in the kitchen. There's nothing quite like college recruiting. There's nothing quite like older, grown men traveling to your town to make a sales pitch to you, a high school kid, or being flown from a place like East Brady to a place like Miami, Florida, where coeds and bikinis were prevalent. It was all pretty crazy.

It's been talked about and written about many times before that I wanted to go to Penn State to play for Joe Paterno. I think every Pennsylvania kid feels this way. You grow up watching the Nittany Lions in the boring (but classic) blue and white uniforms, and you want to be a part of it. I was a pretty good high school basketball player too, and the Penn State coaches came to a few of my high school games. I was pretty sure I was going to be wearing the blue and white. But then one day Penn State called me and said they'd already signed two quarterbacks and that they still wanted me at Penn State. As a linebacker. It didn't take me long to decide that my answer was no. I wanted to play quarterback.

Of course, being Irish Catholic, my folks wanted me to go to Notre Dame. They of course had a great tradition, and culturally South Bend was definitely more like East Brady than Miami, Florida. But when I got to Miami, I saw the beaches, had steak and lobster for the first time in my life, and pretty much just asked "Where do I sign?" My parents were disappointed because they knew they couldn't afford to fly down to Miami for games.

I've made a few decisions in my life that at the time people had trouble understanding. The first was deciding to attend Miami, and the second was deciding to sign with the USFL's Houston Gamblers rather than the Buffalo Bills. Those were both decisions that disappointed some people at the time. But once I make a decision, I go full speed ahead with confidence in that direction, and I don't look back.

At the beginning, at the University of Miami, it was all a little overwhelming. I was a kid from a small town in Pennsylvania, and here I was in this locker room with big-city guys from all over the country. Guys looked different. They talked different. Everything was completely different.

When I first got to Miami, I was in for a number of humbling experiences. For one, I would be running the veer offense, which if you're not familiar is basically the opposite of the pro-style offense that Lou Saban outlined on his recruiting visit. The veer requires a quarterback to be quick on his feet (I wasn't), a runner (again, I wasn't—if you've ever witnessed me run, you know this style offense wasn't suited for me), and make lots of run reads (whether to give to a halfback or run) on the fly. I was a drop-back guy. This wasn't my thing. For a Miami quarterback at that time, your job was to hand off to OJ Anderson, who I would face again in my first Super Bowl when he was starring with the Giants.

OJ was an animal, and we weren't going to be changing an offense that was designed for him. He used to get frustrated that I couldn't get to the edge fast enough to make the pitch to him and told me that I'd "better become a veer quarterback" if I planned to stay at Miami.

College ball is a comedown in lots of other little ways too. For one, I was redshirted, which basically means that Miami was keeping me on the shelf because they had other quarterbacks they felt more comfortable with, including two other freshmen (Mike Rodrigue and Mark Richt, who would go on to fame as Georgia's head coach). The thing about college ball is that every single guy on a college team was not only the star of his high school, but the star of his region or state. Everybody in the locker room can flat-out ball. And to top it off, I wasn't able to get the number I wore in high school (11) or Terry Bradshaw's number (12). I had to settle for 7 because it was the only quarterback's number they had. Just another reminder of my place in the pecking order.

I think there are two kinds of cocky or confidence (for the sake of the chapter title—but truth be told, there's a difference). I was cocky inside . . . in the sense that I knew I could compete and I knew I had what it took. But I wasn't cocky on the outside. If I'd come in there from day one and tried to run the show, it wouldn't have worked out nearly as well. In football if you want to be a leader, you have to earn the respect of the players in your locker room. It's what you say and how you say it, being a good listener and not being quick to judge. Before long, my teammates respected me, and I had confidence that I could lead them.

It's important to remember that Miami wasn't yet fully formed or "branded" as a program. At that time we were a program on the rise, and we didn't have all the swagger that Miami would become famous for in the late 1980s.

I got my first taste of college football against Syracuse in, of all places, Rich Stadium on a cold day in front of about eight thousand people. Coach Saban had left the program before the season, and his replacement was Howard Schnellenberger who, temperament wise, was a much better fit with me. He was more like Terry Henry, my high school coach, in that I felt like I could ask him questions. Still, he was a big, intimidating guy, a drill sergeant, with a "Don't screw with me" kind of demeanor. As such, I didn't screw with him, in any way, shape, or form. Rather, I learned the game of football from him and learned to pass as a result of working with coach Earl Morrall, himself a former NFL quarterback. Morrall taught me to put air under the ball to add distance to an already strong arm. My tendency before had been to throw everything on a rope. He also taught me to carry the ball up by my ear, to add quickness to my release.

We were down 25–7 to Syracuse when Schnellenberger gave me my first opportunity to be a college quarterback. I was as nervous as any nineteen-year-old would be, but I was also excited to show what I could do. I played okay, throwing for 130 yards and a score, and more importantly I built some confidence, feeling like I had what it took to be a big-time college quarterback. The funny thing about confidence is that sometimes you work your way into it, like in my patient work with Morrall, but sometimes you're thrown into the fire and confidence comes as a result.

The next week was business as usual—I was back with the second team at practice, watching somebody else take the first-team reps. But all of that changed four hours before our next game at Penn State, when Coach Schnellenberger informed me that I was the new starter. We had just eaten the pregame meal at the team hotel in State College, PA. I would be starting against the 19th-ranked team in the country, a team that was favored to beat us by about thirty points. The team that didn't want me as a quarterback.

In short, the day was like a dream. It was one of those rare moments as an athlete—and all athletes have them—where nothing could go wrong. I went six for six on our first two series, as we jumped out to a 13–0 halftime lead. We won 26–10, and it was truly one of the best feelings in my entire life. My folks were in the stands, and I couldn't wait to share the victory with the family and friends who had come out to watch me. I threw for 280 yards and three scores, and deep down I had hoped to prove to Joe Paterno that he'd made a mistake.

The rest of that first season was a trial by fire, as we would face Alabama, Notre Dame, and Florida. I suffered a dislocated jaw (against Penn State), a concussion, and cracked ribs. The Alabama and Notre Dame games, both losses, were disasters. I wore the injuries as a badge of courage, like I always did, but deep down my faith and confidence in myself was starting to shake. Almost anybody can play football healthy, but it's when a guy has to play hurt, and play through pain, that his ability and character are truly revealed. And life, like football, gives us plenty of pain.

In our final game, against Florida, I wrapped myself up in a flack jacket and about a mile of athletic tape. It hurt just to take a breath. But I managed to go 10 of 17 for 165 yards and a score, in a 30–24 victory. It was just what I needed going into the off-season, and it was just what our team and program needed, in terms of momentum.

Building Confidence through Facing Fear

Another confidence-related moment came during spring practice of the following season. As you know if you've ever been to Miami, it gets hot there in the spring. Even under the best of conditions, spring ball can be semi-hellish. You're up early in the morning, lifting and running, practicing in the afternoon, and watching film and sitting in meetings the rest of the time with no game on the horizon.

At any rate, the dormitories we were in were air-conditioned, but the AC's were blowing hot air instead of cold. It was like a crematorium in there. One of our offensive linemen had the bright idea that I should talk to Coach Schnellenberger about it. A few thoughts went through my mind. One, I was terrified of Coach, just like everybody was. Two, in football it's important not to look "soft," as in, even if there's a tsunami and a hurricane happening at the same time, nobody wants to be the wuss who decides to come in from practice. Soft is the kiss of death. But my other thought was that this team didn't have a legit veteran leader at any position, and as the quarterback, it was my job to lead the guys into battle. They needed me on the field, and they needed me to man up and walk across campus to the football office to fight this battle. I swallowed hard and walked up the two flights of stairs to the football office. It's amazing that a conversation with a grown man could stir up the kind of nerves I was experiencing. But Schnellenberger's voice could terrify just about anybody.

A word about coaches' offices: everything in the office is there to send a message. Coaches are big on sending a message. The desks are usually always gigantic and oak, and there's always an assortment of memorabilia around meant to sort of intimidate-slash-remind the visitor of where they are in the pecking order of life.

Coach's door was open, and he waved me in. I sat down and quickly made my request. Then I thanked him and got out of there as quickly as possible. The next day there was cold air blowing in our dorm.

———

Coach Schnellenberger really gave a boost to my confidence before my final year of college when he said, "I don't think any one kid has meant as much to a program and its turnaround as Jim Kelly. Pitt was good before Dan Marino. So was Georgia before Herschel Walker. Jim's the most productive quarterback I've been around. And that includes Joe Namath and Ken Stabler. He's the grease that makes our offensive machine run, and our kids have a great deal of confidence in him. Every time he handles the ball, they know they have a chance to score."

Wow. I can't tell you how much that meant. Even after all we'd accomplished as a team, it helped so much to know that I had the faith and confidence of my coach. Truly, none of it would have been possible without Coach Schnellenberger and Coach Morrall.

The Heisman buildup before the 1982 season was crazy, but not as crazy as it could have been. Every postcard, media guide, and letter that went out before the season had the words "Heisman Candidate" next to my name, but I nixed some other ideas, including buttons, T-shirts, and an idea that included sending six packs of oranges stamped with the phrase, "Jim Kelly and oranges, two of Florida's biggest producers." Crazy. I was a football player, not a politician. ABC-TV filmed me on Jet Skis off Miami beach, and a film crew from Philly shot me dressed in a three-piece suit, which was an homage to the fact that I was a business major and that "the University of Miami means business." A newspaper even shot a picture of me in a Heisman pose, in my uniform, in a helmet without a face mask.

One of the biggest single blows to my confidence came at Miami. We were playing in our third game of the season against Virginia Tech, and I pulled the ball down and ran with 12:30 remaining in the fourth quarter. Most quarterbacks slide or run out of bounds, which is exactly what I should have done. It was a third-and-seven play from our own 14-yard line. But in the back of my mind I thought I could score, so I cut back toward the middle of the field and got completely blindsided by a 219-pound defensive end named David Marvel (nickname "Captain"). I landed right on my throwing shoulder, which for a quarterback is just like blowing out a knee for a running back. The throwing arm is your moneymaker, and now mine was seriously compromised. I tried lifting my arm, and it wouldn't budge.

There's something strangely surreal about getting hurt on a football field. Everything slows to a snail's pace, and your senses become weirdly engaged. You feel each blade of grass.

You can hear yourself breathing. You can feel the blood pumping through the part of you that just got hurt. You're no longer thinking about down and distance or your assignment. You're thinking about things like your future, and "Will I ever play again?"

Dr. Joseph Kalbac, our team doc, examined me and rendered his diagnosis as team trainers hovered around. "Total separation of the AC joint," he said. "I'm afraid you're done for the season."

The rest of that night is a blur. I remember my brothers holding ice packs on my shoulder in the locker room. I remember shuffling out without saying a whole lot to the reporters. I remember a guy asking for my autograph, which I thought was pretty ballsy, given the slinged-iced condition of my throwing/writing arm. But I signed for him anyway. Though I would have never said it, I thought it might be my last.

The doctor inserted three metal rods, each about five inches long, into the shoulder to help hold together the ligaments that held together my collarbone and the top of my shoulder blade. Here's the crazy part: they'd be in there for six weeks, and the tips of these rods would actually be sticking right out of the skin on the front of my shoulder. Kind of a horror-movie look.

Kalbac came to my room after the surgery and told me that everything went well. He said it was going to be hard to get my throwing motion back, and then he said, "I sure hope you studied." I'm no student of literature, but the subtext in that statement absolutely floored me. I would never have admitted it then, but I could see my dreams going down the tubes.

Six weeks after they were inserted, the rods came out. The project was every bit as terrifying as it sounds, and it literally involved Kalbec pulling them out with pliers. "I think you'd better give me something to make sure it doesn't hurt," I said. "Trust me, Jim, it's not going to hurt." And it didn't, for a while. But on the third rod, his pliers slipped, and the rod caught a bone. I screamed some words that are better left unsaid.

But then some amazing things happened, and some amazing people rallied around me in Miami. First, my younger brothers moved to Miami to help me rehab and work out, and I never could have done it without them. And then Mike O'Shea and Frank Rice, two UM football trainers, worked with me every day. They pushed me—I can't remember how many times I puked during their workouts—and they told me day in and day out that I was going to make it back to full strength. The amazing thing is that basically my usefulness to the Miami football program was over the moment I went down, but they worked every bit as hard to get me back on the field and ensure that I would have a pro career.

I hung a picture of Mom and Dad in my locker to remind me that I was doing it for them. I wanted to pay them back for all they'd sacrificed for us.

I got to a point where my arm actually felt stronger than it had before the surgery—I think because of all the targeted work I was doing to build it up. But I was still worried that NFL teams would be scared off by the fact that I only played three games my senior year. But Coach Schnellenberger assured me that at whatever point we felt like my arm was 100 percent, he'd call every team in the league and we'd have our own private combine. It's funny, with all the technology available and with all the advances to the game, scouting has changed very little during the years. It's still about scouts showing up and putting their eyes on a player, watching how he moves, watching him make throws.

I remember that day, April 7, 1983, sitting in the locker room at Miami puking my guts out but knowing that I was completely ready to put on a show. Coach Schnellenberger reminded me that I had played in front of huge crowds and national TV audiences, so I had "no reason to be nervous about this." The media dubbed it "Throw for the Dough" and "The Kelly Sweepstakes." Even then, before the NFL Draft became a must-see television event second only to the Super Bowl itself, there was a lot of attention and a lot of spotlight on the Miami practice field. And even then, the difference between first-rounder and second-rounder was hundreds of thousands of dollars.

There were twenty NFL scouts, some representatives from the new United States Football League, and a bunch of legendary coaches there, like Bud Grant and Don Shula. It's kind of intimidating to walk out onto the field and see all of these guys in their team gear there to watch you and only you.

I wore a lucky fishing cap with the words "Charger Power" on it that was given to me at one of the combines by a San Diego Chargers scout. I had worn it on a deep-sea fishing trip earlier, and I hooked a fifty-four pound fish. I thought it might bring me some luck at the workout.

I went out and lit it up—dropping 65 yard bombs right in my receivers' hands and throwing 20 yard comebacks on a rope. I threw 125 passes total, of every variety you can imagine—out patterns, square ins, slants, posts, and go routes.

Shula, the legendary Dolphins coach, left after I threw my first long bomb. Somebody asked him where he was going because he'd only been there like five minutes.

"I've seen enough," he said. "The kid can throw."

Confidence in football and in life is like a roller coaster. Sometimes you're on a high that keeps you focused and energized. But sometimes the lows can be very low. And I guess that's why through all the tragedies and triumphs, the criticism and the praise, I've learned a thing or two about confidence. What it is and what it's not. Bottom line is this— self-confidence will only carry you so far. We all get to the end of ourselves eventually. For some of us (myself included), it takes a little bit longer and a lot more heartbreak. For me, football and those who helped me play the game are what helped shape my confidence and character. But when Hunter got sick, everything changed. I couldn't do anything to help my son get better. No treatment. No cure. My confidence in all that the world had to offer vanished when we received the devastating diagnosis from our doctor. I needed to place my confidence and hope in someone, something greater than myself. Thankfully, God intervened. And over time I learned where true leadership and confidence come from. I'm still a work in progress (that's for sure), but I know where my help and hope come from.

Dear Cam and Erin,

My hope and prayer for you is that you would be confident in Christ. My hope is that your mom and I have backed you with all the love and support you need to go into every situation with confidence—with the confidence

*that no matter what the outcome, you're unconditionally
loved by us. Our hope is that you would lead confidently
but not cockily. That you would prepare diligently, as
unto the Lord. That your peers and teammates would
respect your effort and your heart. That your confidence
wouldn't be tied to performance, but rather to who you are
in Christ.*

Always,
Dad

OFFENSIVE STRATEGIES

1. How have you built confidence in the past? Through slow, patient work, or trials by fire?
2. How would you explain the connection between confidence and leadership?
3. How can people who aren't naturally confident work to build more confidence?
4. How did Jim's coaches help build his confidence?
5. How can you help instill the right kinds of confidence in your kids?
6. Explain the connection between hard work, preparedness, and confidence.

Respect: Earned and Given

Dear Hunter,

It took too long to realize it, but what I always wanted, more than anything, was to be worthy of your respect. I apologize for the ways I failed in that. I have so much respect for the way you lived and for the way you fought hard for life each day. I have so much respect for your mother, for the way that she held our family together all those years. My hope, and my prayer now, is that each day I can earn your sisters' respect as well. Thank you for all that you taught me.

Always,
Daddy

Writing from the office again, where I'm surrounded by golf-shirt samples. There are golf shirts from a bunch of different companies who are vying to be the apparel provider for the annual Jim Kelly Celebrity Golf Tournament. If this seems like a strange way to open a chapter on respect, it is. It's because there's nothing like a celebrity golf tournament to sort of illustrate what's real and what's fake about respect. There's a lot of glad-handing and a false sense of importance at those things. Everybody is "somebody," or everybody is vying for the chance to be near "somebody." It's crazy. But at the end of the day, the tournament raises hundreds of thousands of dollars for Kelly for Kids and Hunter's Hope and Krabbe disease research, so all the hard work is worth it.

A word about money and respect: I'd love to sit here and tell you, all idealistically, that money can't buy respect. And in a way it can't—not the real kind at least. But in a minute I'm going to tell you all about the huge contract I signed when I went to the USFL and the huge house in Houston that I designed, that I just finished showing somebody pictures of today, and, well, in a way you do those things (show pictures, etc.) because you think you need a certain kind of respect. The house in Houston *was* huge (*Sports Illustrated* came down and photographed me in front of a sports car in front of my house), fun (they photographed me in a hot tub and that was back when hot tubs were more about fun and less about just being able to walk around), and I designed it (I used to tell everybody this). And yeah, I guess for a kid from East Brady that was about getting a certain kind of respect or at least promoting a certain kind of image that I thought was cool or important at the time.

And for some people you kind of *can* buy their respect. But it's the kind of respect that comes with all kinds of questions and limitations—the kind that has you questioning everybody's motives all the time because you don't know whether they actually *like* you or they just like the *idea* of you. The idea of you being more about getting their piece of memorabilia signed or getting something for free. It's complicated (respect), but this is why I need at least a few people in my life who will tell me how it is at all times. I respect that in a person. Again, thank God for family and close friends.

The Real Kind of Respect

Football, in a way, is all about getting the real kind of respect. And it seems like just when you've done all you can do to get respect, you have to re-earn it all over again. This is how life seems to work. You're only as good as the last thing you've done. The office, in a way, is full of proof that I've apparently earned this kind of respect . . . and all of that proof is collecting dust. Especially the huge USFL Player of the Year trophy in the corner.

Football can reveal the kinds of things I respect about a person—courage, honor, and the ability to keep one's word. It's the little things, like a firm handshake and making eye contact when you talk with someone. Showing up places on time. Those are the little things that all people can do to earn others' respect. In a football context, especially on a new team or in a new setting, you earn respect by letting your actions do the talking.

As a parent, it's much more of a challenge. You have to gain your kids' respect by being consistent. By letting your yes be yes, and your no be no. Your children need to know that you're trustworthy and capable of keeping your word. And most of all, by loving and caring for your wife. Kids have an innate sense of these things.

And your kids can show their respect—to you and to other authority figures in tangible ways. Things as seemingly little as saying please and thank you, being on time for appointments (this is huge), and looking someone in the eye when they're talking go a long way toward communicating respect. If you challenge your kids in these areas, they will reap the benefit. Adults (other parents, teachers, coaches) will begin to respect your children in new ways, and you'll see that these behaviors will become a way of life for your kids—a way of life that will benefit them down the road in college and in the workplace.

———

Though things had gone well at my invitation-only audition in Miami, I had no idea what to expect on NFL Draft day, which was April 26, 1983. As I write this, the NFL Draft is a full-blown made-for-television event, as are all the events (combine, pro days) leading up to the draft. It's like the capitalist Olympics—lots of fit, young, hungry guys running, lifting, and jumping for money. In 1983 I felt like I'd done all I could have done to earn the respect of the league leading up to draft day. Deep down, I really wanted to be a Steeler or a Raider—my two favorite teams at the time.

John Elway was the first quarterback drafted in a class that would eventually go down in history as one of the best for quarterbacks of all time. Elway was drafted by the Baltimore Colts, who at the time were a franchise in disarray. He brokered a trade to the Denver Broncos and the rest, as they say, is history. We faced each other many times, and I have a great deal of respect for John. After John went, the next quarterback drafted was Todd Blackledge, a Penn Stater, who went to the Chiefs.

I was praying that the Bills wouldn't draft me. I guess I didn't have a whole lot of respect for the Bills at the time. They had just lost a strong coach, Chuck Knox, and after getting accustomed to south Florida, I wasn't excited about playing and living in the snow. As a kid I had closed my eyes and imagined playing in the Steelers' black and gold. Granted, Terry Bradshaw was still there, but he figured to be retiring soon, and I couldn't think of anyone else I'd rather sit behind for a year or two than my childhood hero.

Buffalo had two opportunities to grab me—in the twelfth and fourteenth spots. I remember literally screaming, immaturely, "No, please don't take me!!" In retrospect I feel pretty ashamed of that. I mean, I had the audacity to be picky about how and where I would live out the dreams of every kid who has ever put on a football helmet. When NFL commissioner Pete Rozelle stepped to the podium and said, "With the fourteenth pick, the Buffalo Bills select Miami quarterback Jim Kelly," I let out a groan. I had a fundamental problem with the idea that somebody else could choose where I would live and make my living. It was a weird position to be in—fulfilling a dream, but at the same time being supremely bummed out by how it was playing out.

I had some options though, including the USFL. The United States Football League was conceived by David Dixon, who saw an opportunity to take advantage of football-crazy fans while the NFL was in its off-season. The USFL started with some serious financial backing and was making a run at big-time players. It felt like a viable option at the time. I had already been drafted by the USFL's Chicago Blitz. The upside to the Blitz is that they were coached by coaching legend George Allen. The downside is that they played in Chicago and struggled to draw even smallish crowds in Soldier Field.

Meanwhile, the situation in Buffalo was really dire, and none of the top picks that year—including Notre Dame tight end Tony Hunter and West Virginia linebacker Darryl Talley—really wanted to be there. Still, the Bills did their best to roll out the red carpet for me and recruit me to sign there. Kay Stephenson, the head coach, even let me use his car to drive home from minicamp to see my mom, who was struggling with emphysema. Minicamp was an odd sensation—having to climb up on a podium to give press conferences (not to mention practice) with a team I really had no intention of playing for. And what's worse, incumbent quarterback Joe Ferguson (who was a really solid NFL quarterback and an incredibly hard worker) had my jersey number. It felt like a bad omen.

My agents and I were being wined and dined by the USFL. The late John Bassett, owner of the USFL's Tampa Bay Bandits, invited us to his condo and to a Bandits game to get a feel for the quality of play in the USFL. Quality of play aside (and I was impressed with it), it was great to be back in Florida. There were yachting expeditions and barbecues on the beach. I didn't want to leave. This is a good time to add what a mind-blower it was to have all of these teams and owners vying for my attention. In retrospect, I doubt that this kind of attention can be good for a young guy's character . . . but I won't lie, it was fun.

My agents were close to making a deal with the Bills, but what finally happened is this: we got an eleventh-hour offer from the USFL, basically saying that I could have my pick of *any* franchise in the league. The USFL was trying to make a run at high-profile players, and George Allen, who owned my rights, basically gave that up for the good of advancing the profile of the league. And what's more, my best friend Mark

Rush (who had been drafted by the Vikings in the fourth round) was a part of the package deal. We could choose any team and go there together. It was a dream come true. So Mark and I sat down and hashed out our list of "dream" franchises, all of which were in warm-weather climates.

Houston Gamblers owner Jerry Argovitz invited Mark and me down for what was part recruiting trip and part tryout. He showed us all over Houston, took us to some great restaurants, and introduced us to some of the city's high rollers. Houston had a lot going for it—namely the fact that it played in a domed stadium, which is a quarterback's dream. In a dome conditions are perfect—it's always warm and windless.

Jerry also wanted to see for himself, apparently, how lively my arm was after the surgery. So much so that he decided to run some routes himself and encouraged me to put as much zip as I could on the ball. I put enough zip on it to break his right ring finger. I guess he saw enough. The next day he offered me $3.5 million over five years, with a $1 million signing bonus. The Bills weren't about to match that amount, but then again, the Gamblers and the USFL were trying to make a big splash—they were looking for the kind of move that the AFL made when they signed Joe Namath.

My dad wanted me to play with the Bills because it was closer to East Brady, but as in all decisions I knew my parents would support me and have my back.

When Mark and I signed with the Houston Gamblers, they had a grand total of three players on the roster—Jim Kelly, Mark Rush, and a linebacker named Kiki DeAyala. I didn't know what kind of offense they ran because they didn't have a coach. What I did know, for a fact, was that I had a real check for $200,000 in my pocket—the first installment of my million-dollar signing bonus. After the press conference, Mark and I went to the bank and got a couple thousand dollars, which we then literally spread out all over the beds in our hotel room, like little kids. We thought we were rich. It all sounds so ridiculous now, and since this chapter is about respect—sort of disrespectful as well, but that was then. It was a wild ride for a kid from East Brady.

———

When I first watched film on the run-and-shoot offense, I knew I was going to have to work on my footwork. I was a traditional drop back, pocket passer, and the run and shoot was predicated on the quarterback taking the snap from center and sprinting out—meaning that I would take like a half-roll to either side of the field on almost every play. I also knew I was going to take a beating because leaving the pocket leaves a quarterback vulnerable. I also never had what you would call "blazing" foot speed. I was never a 4.7 40-yard dash guy. I got to 4.85 once, but that was on Astroturf with about a 5–10 mph tailwind behind me.

But at the same time I knew what a great opportunity it was to throw the ball a ton, which every quarterback loves to do. I also knew that it would help me read coverages because I would be reading on the run. Mouse Davis, who was the architect of the run and shoot and was our offensive coordinator, helped me tremendously with my footwork, and I would stay after practice almost every day to do agility drills and run gassers—pretty much anything to prepare me for what I was about to do. Mouse was a great teacher and always kept the game fun.

The way the run and shoot worked is that the basic formation consisted of four wide receivers, a running back, and no
tight ends. Each receiver had three to five choices depending
on how the defense was lined up across from him. Basically
once the ball was snapped, everybody was reading on the run,
and the hope was that everybody was reading the right things
at the right times. In the run and shoot, you're often throwing
on your fourth or sixth step—as opposed to a three-, five-, or
seven-step drop in a standard offense. You almost never know
where the ball is going to go when you get to the line of scrimmage, so you have to be ready to take advantage of an opportunity when it arises.

I also felt comfortable going to the USFL because so many
top-flight guys—like Herschel Walker, Mike Rozier, Doug
Flutie, and Steve Young—had decided to make the jump
before me. The USFL, as a league, was getting the respect of
the football community. And the USFL allowed me to suit up
against some of pro football's all-time greats.

My rookie year with Houston I got to face future NFL
Hall of Famer Steve Young and the LA Express in the Astro-
dome. They compared our game to the "Shootout at the OK
Corral" because both offenses were so good at scoring points.
Our receivers were all tiny, but they were all so quick. We
called them "The Mouseketeers." We had guys like Clarence
Verdin and Ricky Sanders, who would go on to star for the
Colts and the Redskins, respectively.

The fans loved us in Houston. We had these great black
uniforms—with black helmets and black jerseys with a picture of the outline of Texas—and what was even better was
that we scored a bunch of points and won ball games. They

loved our coach, Jack Pardee, as well. He was an all-American as a linebacker at Texas A&M and went on to have a long career in the NFL. He was a tough, hard-nosed leader and was named NFL Coach of the Year in 1979 with the Redskins.

We didn't have a tight end on our roster, and we rarely ran the ball. When we ran, we ran sprint draws that always confused the defense. Coming into our game with the Express, we were averaging more than 400 yards per game and 33 points per game.

We capped the opening drive of the game with a touchdown pass to Richard Johnson, who was leading the entire USFL in receiving. On the play, I sprinted out to my right and threw back across my body to my left, which is a tough throw for any quarterback to make.

The Express roster, just like ours, was loaded with NFL-caliber talent. They had a corner, Wymon Henderson, who would go on to start in a couple of Super Bowls with the Broncos, as well as Mel Gray, Jo-Jo Townsell, and Freddie Scott, who had spent ten years with the Lions and Colts. And Young was such a great athlete in those days. The week before he played us, he had more than 400 yards of total offense himself, including 120 yards rushing. On his first drive he hurt us with his arm and his legs. He answered with his own touchdown pass to Tony Boddie.

In the second quarter, on a sprint out, I was hit on my right arm and fumbled—a fumble that was recovered for a touchdown by a guy named Eddie "The Meat Cleaver" Weaver. USFL nicknames were nothing if not colorful. We drove the ball down later to tie the score at 14 when I hit Clarence Verdin for a touchdown.

By the end of the third quarter, the Express cornerbacks were giving our receivers a huge cushion (meaning, they were playing a good fifteen yards off the line of scrimmage), and we nickeled-and-dimed our way down the field, hitting quick outs and hitch routes. We had a receiver named Gerald McNeil, who was 5'8" and 140 pounds. I hit him on a crossing route on the last play of the third quarter, and he got absolutely blasted by Dwight Drane, who was about 6' and 200 pounds. McNeil bounced off the turf but held onto the ball. That's why fans loved us, and why I loved The Mouseketeers.

And believe it or not we ended that drive on, of all things, an option play. I took the snap and ran to the right, down the line of scrimmage, before pitching to Todd Fowler, who ran the ball in for the score. It felt like high school...or my first year at Miami. If only OJ Anderson could have seen me then. That drive was a great example of how fun it was to play in the USFL. I had a great time there, and I think it only raised my stock in the eyes of the NFL, where I probably wouldn't have played right away as a rookie and where I definitely wouldn't have put up the kind of numbers I put up in the USFL.

I finished that rookie year with some gaudy statistics, which were mostly attributable to Mouse Davis's offense. In the regular season I passed for 5,219 yards and 44 touchdowns. Until Dan Marino tossed 48 for the Dolphins, that was a record for most TD passes in a season in all of professional football. The high point came when we got to travel to Pittsburgh to take on the Maulers in Three Rivers Stadium. I passed for five touchdown passes in a 47–26 victory, on Mother's Day. I told St. Alice that all the touchdown passes were for her.

By my second year, the league's financial troubles were starting to catch up to the Gamblers. There were weeks when our game checks were late. Finally, the Gamblers merged with Donald Trump's New Jersey Generals, and I thought I would be playing my third USFL season in New Jersey with Herschel Walker in what was being called a "dream" backfield. We even had a few minicamp practices together. However, even though the USFL "won" its antitrust lawsuit against the NFL, it was rewarded a measly three bucks. Not exactly enough to keep game checks rolling in on time. There would never be another USFL season.

I played my first ever NFL preseason game in 1986 against the defending Super Bowl champion Chicago Bears and Buddy Ryan's 46 defense in which he sent blitzers from everywhere and almost killed a lot of quarterbacks. The footage of that defense, in '85, was legendary. I remember seeing Bears linebacker Wilber Marshall almost kill Lions quarterback Eric Hipple in the Pontiac Silverdome. Marshall blasted him, and for a second they thought Hipple was dead. He just went limp like a rag doll when his head hit the Astroturf. Nothing like starting out easy.

The game was played at Notre Dame Stadium in South Bend, in what seemed like 100-degree heat and 100-percent humidity. People, don't underestimate how hot it gets in the Midwest in August. I had just signed an $8 million contract and had thrown for almost 10,000 yards and 83 touchdown passes in the USFL, so to say that the pressure was on would be an understatement. Media types were calling me "the eight-million-dollar man." I had signed on August 14th, just a few days previous, and had stepped out of a private jet and into a small press conference on the tarmac where I held up my jersey for reporters. I was then taken, by limousine, to Bills headquarters. Three years ago when the Bills drafted me, I cried. Now I was signing with them.

I looked out the limo window during the ride to the complex and couldn't believe what I was seeing. There were people holding up signs that said "Welcome Back, Jim" and "We Love You." This was a team that had gone 2-14 in 1984 and again in 1985, when they averaged 37,000 fans per game in a stadium that seated 80,000. Four times in 1985 they had fewer than 30,000 fans show up. I had my work cut out for me.

I was twenty-six years old, already several years out of college, and a grown man. I thought of myself as a leader, and everybody expected me to lead that team. Personally, I think that team needed an attitude adjustment—we needed to believe that we could win and we needed to get the respect of the league. I was excited and nervous knowing we were going against the defending Super Bowl champs.

And sometimes I made things harder on myself. When I was with the Houston Gamblers the year before, I had remarked that we could score at least five touchdowns on the Bears defense. At the time it hadn't occurred to me how a statement like that could come back to haunt me. Otis Wilson, the Bears outside linebacker said that they "didn't forget." Wilson was known for his pass rush off the edge, and also for barking like a dog when he got angry. This is a little disconcerting. The Bears had a ton of Hall of Fame type talent on that defense, including Mike Singletary, Wilber Marshall,

Dan Hampton, Steve McMichael, Richard Dent, and William Perry who had a superfast first step for a guy who weighed 325 pounds. When I first came into the league, 300-pounders were few and far between, but when I left, athletic 300-pounders were a dime a dozen.

I threw up in the locker room before the game, but, truth be told, I threw up before almost every game. Football meant so much to me that I had a huge amount of anxiety before each game. I knew I could perform, but I was afraid of letting anyone down.

I came in during the first half to an eruption of boos from the crowd. Buffalo fans are tough, Philly fans are probably sociopathic, but Chicago fans are somewhere in between. My first NFL preseason pass was a completion to running back Ronnie Harmon, who was our first-draft choice that season and was a very solid receiver out of the backfield. Otis Wilson unloaded on me on one of the last plays in the first quarter. He came in unblocked on a blitz and gave me my first bona fide NFL bell ringer. There would be many more.

Getting hurt and playing hurt is a way of life in football, especially in the NFL. When I hurt my shoulder at Miami in college, as I was lying on the field, my brother Danny came up to me and said, "You're a Kelly, you'll be fine." At face value that's one of those false-bravado, self-congratulatory, say-it-in-the-heat-of-the-moment-to-feel-better sort of things, but there was really some truth to it. What he meant was, "You're a Kelly, so I know you'll do everything in your power to get back to full strength as quickly as you can."

He was right, in a way. My brothers have been in locker rooms with me through all kinds of injuries—concussions, turf burns, shoulder separations, and all kinds of contusions. The fact of the matter is that the scariest, and toughest, guys I ever squared off against were my brothers. Everything else has seemed just a little bit easier, by comparison. There are six of us, and I'm the third youngest—Pat (61), Ed (57), Ray (54), myself, Danny (50), and Kevin (50).

Signing with the Buffalo Bills in 1986 was one of the best decisions I ever made. The city was special, which is one reason why I still live there, and the fans were even better. It was a real college-type environment at Rich Stadium (now Ralph Wilson Stadium) on a Bills game day. Fans would roll up, sometimes the night before, in their RVs and tailgate all day and night. The stadium itself was located right in the middle of a small town. It's like you had all of these neighborhood bars, houses, and then Rich Stadium. And the fans were up close, right on top of the field. Needless to say, it was a tough place to play for our opponents, especially when it was snowing or sleeting or the wind was blowing (which seemed like all the time). According to the chamber of commerce, we averaged something like 93 inches of snow per year—most of it, I think, came during Bills playoff games.

The atmosphere was pretty electric when we opened the 1986 season at home against the Jets. The 79,951 people in the stands gave the Bills their first sellout in three years, and the game would be nationally televised. Apparently being the highest-paid player in the NFL comes with some attention. I felt like the expectations were sky-high—there were signs all over the stadium about me being some kind of savior and expecting me in one fell swoop to turn around the city of Buffalo in addition to the Bills. It was crazy.

We were wearing our all-white uniforms, and I couldn't hear myself think as I ran out of the tunnel, with almost 80,000 people screaming in unison. I'll never forget it.

Somebody made a sign out of a bed sheet that read, "Kelly Is God." Insane.

When I went into the huddle for our first series, I honestly just wanted to get the play called, handle the snap correctly, and get positive yardage. My first NFL pass was a completion to tight end Pete Metzelaars on a play-action pass. I would hit Pete later on that series, as well as do some scrambling. The crowd noise was almost deafening.

You couldn't have scripted my first series as a Bill any better. We had a good running back named Greg Bell who mixed in a couple of nice runs and who ultimately caught my first touchdown pass as a Bill to end that drive. I pumped my fist at the crowd when I got to the sideline, which was something I would do many, many times before it was all said and done.

The Jets had a great team, and many people were picking them to go to the Super Bowl. Their quarterback, Ken O'Brien, was a classmate of mine from the '83 draft. He hit Al Toon for a 46-yard touchdown to make it 14–7. They had an aggressive defensive line too. Their great nose tackle Joe Klecko jumped offsides in the second quarter and knocked me right off my feet. I got welcomed to the NFL just before halftime, courtesy of a shot from Mark Gastineau that left me semiconscious. For some reason I thought we were back in Pittsburgh instead of Buffalo. By the time I got to the huddle, I had forgotten the play, and Greg Bell had to bail me out by calling another one before we got a delay-of-game penalty.

Just before halftime we mounted a drive that ended in a

Scott Norwood field goal. Even though he was only in his second year out of tiny Kutztown University, I was already developing some rapport with Andre Reed. Reed was a Pennsylvania product as well, and I knew he had the speed and toughness to excel in the league. Andre made his living going across the middle, and I hit him on a crossing route with a minute gone in the fourth quarter. He did the rest, taking it 55 yards for the score.

I scrambled and hit Jerry Butler, and then on the next play hit Pete Metzelaars (again) to put us inside the five. Metzelaars played at tiny Wabash College in Indiana. They play Division III football there, and it's an all-guy's school. I don't know how he survived it! But I'm glad our personnel guys found him. On the very next play, I fell on my butt as soon as I got the snap because Jim Ritcher stepped on my foot! I got up, rolled back and right, with what seemed like the whole Jets defense giving chase. I pumped and lofted up a prayer to the back of the end zone, where Metzellaars came down with it. Al Toon would win it for them with a touchdown with only a minute to go in the game. The game would end with the score 28–24, Jets.

I became the first Bills quarterback since Joe Ferguson in 1983 to throw for three TD's in a game and was establishing myself as the leader of our team.

The Bills Earn Respect

We won twelve games and a division championship in 1988, and expectations were high for the 1989 season.

On September 10, 1989, we played the Dolphins in Miami.

It was the opening day of the season and was one of those Miami afternoons that was just oppressively wet-blanket hot. But we always played well in Joe Robbie Stadium—so well, in fact, that we called it Rich Stadium South. There's also the fact that I think half of upstate New York ends up relocating to south Florida at some point, so we always had a fan base down there. There was just a comfort level there, for some reason, and I was used to the hot weather from my time at The U. As used to it as a northern kid can be.

We were down 24–20 with 1:52 to go and got a huge pick from Nate Odomes who was playing Mark Duper (and his retro face mask) to the inside on a post. It was his second interception of the game, and the Dolphins, who lived by the pass, also sometimes died by it when they couldn't close games like this out on the ground. Dan Marino, who it should be noted that I have a ton of respect for, had Jim Jensen, the quintessential Gritty White Guy, open in the flat but elected to go downfield, and Nate made him pay big-time.

Anyway, we had a minute and a half to go, and the announcers kept saying that I needed to throw the ball out of bounds or something to stop the clock because we didn't have time-outs and I was taking up too much time. However, sometimes announcers fail to know what the heck they're talking about. I hit Chris Burkett, Thurman Thomas, Burkett again...threw one incompletion...and then hit Andre Reed. In the pantheon of great receivers, Andre sometimes gets overlooked because he didn't run his mouth and self-promote like many of his more famous contemporaries. But he was every bit as good, if not better, than all of them, and his catch on this drive was beyond clutch. He went up in a crowd and came down with a high pass. The only problem was that he was in the middle of the field and the clock was still running. When he came down with the ball, there were sixteen ticks left on the clock, and it looked like everybody was moving in slow motion because it was the fourth quarter. Thurman, in particular, wandered back to his running-back position like he was taking a walk in the park. Great athletes, like Thurman, always make everything look easy.

The crowd was going berserk, Marv was going berserk, and pretty much everybody else except the eleven Buffalo Bills on the field. We got up to the line of scrimmage, and I drilled the ball into the ground to stop the clock with two ticks. Marv was going nuts because one of their linemen was in our backfield when I snapped the ball, so we got an offsides penalty out of the deal as well. Half the distance to the goal line.

We came to the line of scrimmage in a shotgun (of course) with Ronnie Harmon to my right, two wideouts, a tight end flexed to the right in a two-point stance and a flanker on his inside shoulder. It looked, to all the world, like we were going to throw. In fact, we had called a pass in the flat to Ronnie Harmon, but I noticed the Dolphins' rookie free safety Louis Oliver drifting to the outside, and as soon as I saw that, I said to myself, "I'm going for it." If you watch the tape of that game, you'll notice that Marv wasn't even wearing a headset. One of the things I loved about that guy and his leadership style was that he always let his players play and his leaders lead. He and offensive coordinator Ted Marchibroda trusted me to run that offense. Before the game that week, Ted called me one of the toughest competitors he'd ever coached.

I took the snap, took a couple of steps back, and then ran right up the middle off the block of Kent Hull, my center, and guard Jim Ritcher. I dove across the goal line with a Miami linebacker wrapped around my legs and Oliver ramming his helmet into my hip. We won the game, and I would soon be dog-piled by about 2,000 pounds of celebrating Buffalo Bills. Weirdly, our fans were going nuts in the background, and it sounded like Rich Stadium for a minute. Their legendary coach Don Shula just walked off the field with his head down and went straight to the locker room while our sideline sprinted onto the field and celebrated. I read later that Shula had tears streaming down his face when he entered the locker room.

But I knew, for a fact, that the Bills had started to earn some respect.

I've learned a lot since my NFL days. I've learned that respect is more about others than about yourself. It's not so much about what is deserved but rather what is selflessly given. It's about people. Treating others as you would want to be treated.

Dear Cam and Erin,

Respect is such a two-way street. On one hand, my hope and prayer is that the people in your life— classmates, coworkers, and potential spouses—would always honor and respect you. You'll have to earn their respect by working hard and making wise decisions. Right now I'm around to make sure people show you respect, but soon you'll have to do that on your own. And my other

hope is that you would always show respect—in your
words to others and in your deeds.

Always,
Dad

OFFENSIVE STRATEGIES

1. What are some of the tangible ways to show respect to the people in your life? Parents? Coworkers? Supervisors?
2. As a leader, how do you earn the respect of the people you're leading?
3. As a parent, how are you earning the respect of your children?
4. How are you encouraging your children to cultivate self-respect?

Preparation: Keep Slingin' It, Twelve

Dear Hunter,

I always gave everything I had to play the game of football. I watched a lot of film, ran a lot of stadium steps, and was always prepared to do what I needed to do. But nothing in the world could prepare me for what God did for us through you. And nothing could prepare me for the wild ride of being a parent. I thank God for you, buddy.

Always,
Your dad

I was never a guy who liked to run a lot of wind sprints. In fact, I never liked to run distance at all. People come up to me now, in retirement, and say "Jim, you still running?" and I say something like, "No way—I didn't run that much when I played." In the NFL you run as a group, so you have your teammates there to encourage you and push you along and help you prepare. But I never really liked it. People like to lift—everybody likes the feeling they get from being in the weight room and seeing their body change—but running was much tougher.

My favorite thing to do was stadium steps. I would go into Rich Stadium with the Bills strength and conditioning coach Rusty Jones, who was always there with me to push me and work out with me. And there was just something, too, about being able to work out in the stadium that we played in. I always liked being there and liked visualizing how the hard work would pay off on the field. There was a lot in it for Rusty too, though. He knew that as the Bills did well on the field, he did well and got paid, so there was a clause in my contract that I had to work out a specific number of days each off-season. But to be honest, they didn't even need the clause—I would have been there anyway, and I know my teammates felt the same way.

The Value of Mental Preparation

The physical part of preparation was always a lot tougher than the mental part. For example, I was one of the first players in the league to have a Betacam film system on hand at my house, for film-watching purposes. Now, granted, I wasn't like Peyton Manning—who watches thousands of hours of film each season and is like a PhD on the field. But I looked for trends in the defense, and it was one of the ways that I got prepared to run the K-Gun offense. In the K-Gun, I had to come to the line of scrimmage and make calls and decisions in an instant, within seconds. So the more thinking I could do at home, in front of the projector, the better.

I looked for every trend I could find in the defense . . . what they did on first and ten, what they did on third and long, and what they did in the red zone. Our film department would break them up by reel—so I'd have a short-yardage reel, a red-zone reel, and a third-and-long reel. I would look at sight adjustments on blitz packages, which means that if the defense was showing blitz, I had to know that my receiver was going to read it too and be where he needed to be.

During the years I learned almost every "tell" that a defensive back could give. If a strong safety was in man coverage, most likely he lined up head up over the tight end. Chances are if he was blitzing, the safety would creep up a little bit closer to the line of scrimmage. In the running game, I'd look to see if the nose tackle was shaded one way or another. I knew what plays I wanted to run in a given situation, but there are so many things that come into your mind. If you start thinking too much, you're done. I had to make sure my mind and body were just reacting to the situations they'd been given.

In the K-Gun we would really only huddle before the first play in a drive. I had a pretty good idea of what my first few calls were going to be, but I would only give the first one in the huddle. Before calling that first play, I'd always try to say something motivational to the guys, to try to set some kind of a tone for the rest of the game.

At the line of scrimmage I would always look at the secondary to see what kind of coverage they were in—a three-deep zone (meaning three deep safeties), a two-deep zone, or man-to-man coverage. If we had a running play called, I would check the defensive front and the coverage.

In between plays I had about thirty seconds to drag myself off the turf (sometimes), check out the down and distance, and make this kind of call: First, I'd call out a number, like the number "8" which meant a formation with the tight end to the right, our wide receiver Don Beebe on the right, Andre Reed in the slot on the left, and then James Lofton split out wide to the left. This was all done at the line of scrimmage. We didn't huddle, so everybody had to be prepared and paying attention. I would then call out a name like "Cubs," "Bears," or "Flood." This told the offensive line which protection we were in—which just means that they would slide a certain way or have certain responsibilities in blitz pickup. Then I would call out a number like "93," which would tell every receiver what they were doing on a given play. All of the wide-outs, slot guys, running backs, and tight ends would know what to do. Then, finally, I'd call out a snap count. When I said "Noah," it meant we were going on two huts. "Louis-ville" meant the play was on three. We picked Louisville because one of our offensive linemen, Will Wolford, was from there.

We had a nose tackle in Buffalo named Fred Smerlas who went to the New England Patriots. We knew Fred knew what our cadence calls were, and we knew that he told his guys. So when we played the Patriots I told the guys to go on "Noah," which was usually two-huts, but that day we went on three-huts on Noah. Smerlas was offsides and in my backfield all day. His plan failed.

Truth be told, because of all the concussions, I have trouble with my memory at times. I can say to Jill, "Let's go see *Inception*," to which she'll reply, "Jim, we saw that a few weeks ago." It's a little scary, honestly. But the weird thing is that I can remember almost every piece of terminology that I used in almost every offense I played in. The terminology for play calls at the line of scrimmage would change every week so that teams couldn't pick up on what we were doing from week to week. The terminology becomes so ingrained because of the mind/body connection. You use the words and run the plays so often that they're forever imbedded in your subconscious. I can even remember the plays I called in high school.

Football is a physical game, but it's mentally challenging as well. We ran the K-Gun in practice all the time so that running it became like second nature to us. It was a fast-paced offense, and when we started using it all the time, we scored. And we won. A lot.

The Value of Routine

My game-day ritual was the same before every game. I had to have the same Buffalo Bills trainer, Eddie Abramoski, tape my ankles. If you've ever played football, you know that there's something semimagical about a good tape job, and conversely there's something indescribably terrible about a bad one. The tape sometimes just cuts into your skin in aggravating ways. That's not to say that all of our trainers couldn't have given me great tape jobs; I just got used to Eddie's—he's in the National Trainers Hall of Fame—so why not have the best?

I would always put my right thigh pad in my game pants before my left thigh pad. And I always laced up my rib protector with the same black shoelace, starting from bottom to top. Sometimes I would rip my locker to pieces looking for that black string. And if I happened to walk out to the field before putting my wristbands on, I just got a bad feeling about the rest of the day—even if I went back in to grab them.

And I tried to enjoy the vibe in the locker room before games. An NFL locker room is a special place. We had the best of everything—uniforms, facilities, and athletes. And believe it or not, it's the little things—like putting my thigh pads in my shiny white game pants—that I miss the most. I'll never get to do that again, and honestly it kind of bums me out. I'll never get to walk into the giant opening at the base of Rich Stadium for players and then walk down the concrete tunnel into the door marked "Bills Personnel Only." That door always has a poster of the NFL uniform regulations next to it. Stuff like how long your socks have to be and how much color they have to have showing. The NFL has people—usually ex-players—who they pay to enforce these uniform regulations.

I'll never walk in to see the blue game jerseys and red game helmets all hanging, perfectly, in each guy's locker. I'll never feel what it's like to walk in my taped, bare feet across the carpet in the locker room. Or see the piles of tape and jerseys on the floor of the locker room after a game. These are some of the little things you miss and some of the things that make football such a special game.

I used to room with Frank Reich before games. Frank was a cerebral guy, and we would watch a lot of film together to find tendencies in the defense and he was my coach on the sidelines. And then he would always order us two milkshakes from room service. Every time. "Frankie J" would order vanilla, and I would always order chocolate. Memories.

If we were at home, I would go from the hotel to my house to spend some time with my family before the game. Games were always like family reunions for the Kellys, and there would be a huge assortment of people at the house. I loved this. And I never forgot what a tremendous privilege it was to be able to have them in the stands, watching me play the game we dreamed about so much as kids. Sometimes I would go to pregame mass with Father Fran. To be honest, and this is no disrespect to Father Fran, I couldn't tell you anything that was ever said in any pregame mass because by that time my mind was always on my work and the nerves were already starting to build. Knees were jiggling. Palms were sweating. Plays were being reviewed and rereviewed in my head.

When I was dressed in my uniform, I would always go out to warm up with wide receiver and special teams ace, Steve Tasker, who would always, without fail, say to me, "Keep slingin' it, twelve." Every time. Very matter-of-factly. People think NFL players are always hitting each other in the face or head butting lockers or jumping around like crazy to get ready, but when Steve said that to me before games, it reassured me that he was ready. And it also just reminded me how cool it was to get to play the game with my friends. The relational part of the game always meant a ton to me.

There was nothing like walking down the tunnel with Tasker to warm up. At the field end of the tunnel, you could see the goalpost, the net behind the goalpost, and then the expanse of green Astroturf field beyond it. On either side of the tunnel were Bills fans lined up for autographs or high fives. After throwing balls to Tasker and a few others—getting a feel for the wind in the stadium, the condition of the turf, and the feel of the game balls—I would always look for a little kid with my number on and toss him the ball that we had warmed up with.

A word about game balls: in the NFL they use brand new balls for each game. The balls came out of a box, and the equipment guys inflated them to the right weight. They also came with a sheen of oil on them, and the equipment guys would rub this off with towels so that the balls were grippable and throwable. Every quarterback had a different opinion as to how much of this rubbing should take place and who among the equipment staff should be doing the rubbing. This was part superstition and part legitimate game preparation.

Guys were particular about their jerseys as well. I always kind of had them cut my arm holes at an angle so that I would have the most mobility possible for throwing. But there were linemen, like Will Wolford, who would use double-sided carpet tape to make their jerseys as tight as humanly possible. Like painted-on tight. Getting the jerseys on was a pretty elaborate process that involved multiple ball boys, but our equipment manager, Woody, would do it for every lineman and linebacker every week. And these cheapskates would only pay him five bucks a week! And some of these linemen didn't exactly have physiques on which the painted-on look was flattering. But they felt like it gave them an edge, and they were probably right. A lineman is more dangerous if he can't be grabbed by his jersey or pads.

But the receivers (except for Tasker) were most particular about their uniforms. Their knee pads and thigh pads had to be as small and nonexistent as possible, while still being within the rules. This meant that their knee pads were just little pieces of foam about a half-inch thick and maybe two inches by two inches in diameter. Their thigh pads were actually just the little piece of plastic that came in between the foam padding in a regular thigh pad. The equipment guys would cut them open with X-ACTO knives and extract the piece of plastic, which would then go into the wide receiver's game pants. Receivers would sacrifice protection for speed and vanity.

Before almost every game, the equipment guys would redo all of the hardware on our helmets and put on new logos and decals. They would check all of the straps on our pads and make sure everything was new and working perfectly. The NFL is a well-oiled machine, and nothing happens without a bunch of prepared people working together perfectly. Everybody has a responsibility and a job to do. Randy "Woody" Ribbeck (who stills works for the team) was the best. He was the man and took care of me from the moment I walked into the locker room until this very day.

Preparation for the Game of Life

Preparation is very much the same in life. Every night my dad would lay out his work stuff for the next day. His cereal bowl. His clothes for work. He was prepared. That's the kind of thing you notice as a kid and the kind of thing that stays with you. With my kids I try to teach them the importance of not letting things go until the last minute.

Whether my girls are doing homework or getting ready to play a basketball game, it's important that they're prepared ahead of time and not waiting until the last minute to start focusing on what they need to do.

With the Bills we stressed the importance of making good use of your warm-up. Run the routes you're going to run in the game. Make sure you know the field conditions, the direction of the wind, and the overall feel of the environment.

Sometimes I get frustrated when I see my daughters gabbing with their friends before a game. I know they're just having fun, and at one level I love that, but at the same time, they need to begin preparing themselves mentally for the task at hand.

Football-wise, practice was an interesting mix of coming to learn and coming to prove or show what you'd already learned. Especially at the NFL level, our coaches expected us to come with an understanding of the basics of the offense, but we were also there to learn, and in a way we were "life-long learners" in that every week and every new defense presented a new challenge for us.

And recently I'm learning that our spiritual lives are no different. We're always learning, yet we're striving to live lives that show a respect for, and a growing knowledge of, our Lord. That's why church is important and why accountability is important. Just like my Bills teammates kept me accountable when it came to running and preparation, the pastors and counselors at our church make sure we're striving to live lives that glorify God, even though we're sinners and will never be perfect. I'm still a work in progress and will be until I see God.

Prayer also prepares me to face the many uncertainties of life. I think Hunter taught all of us how to pray. We always had to be prepared because we never knew what each day would hold for our little soldier. But, truth is, God was the only one that really knew and still knows what each day will bring. It's all about trusting Him more with all of our moments.

I would throw up in the locker room before almost every game. It became a ritual of sorts. I would hole up in a stall and wait to throw up. It (the throwing up) was a mixture of nerves and excitement. I knew that every time I walked out there I might not come back in one piece. My breathing would get shallow, and I'd concentrate on a spot on the stall. I'd close my eyes . . . and then I'd throw up. That's when I knew I was fully prepared.

I always walked out of the locker room and down the tunnel with my offensive linemen. I'd been doing that ever since the University of Miami. Sometimes my linemen wouldn't leave the locker room if I hadn't puked yet. Even they knew that it was the universal sign for "Jim's ready." Truth be told, sometimes I faked throwing up just to get them to leave the locker room.

Dear Cam and Erin,

 Preparation was a huge part of my life as an NFL player. How you prepare as an athlete often makes or breaks your experience. Life is no different. The way that you prepare for school, for friendships, and for the things that will come your way in life make all the difference. We're given great responsibility in life, and with it comes the need to prepare. My prayer for you is that you would be thoughtful and intentional in your preparation for life's responsibilities.

Love,
Dad

OFFENSIVE STRATEGIES

1. How do you prepare for the key events in your life?
2. Why is preparation critical not only in the big events but in the day-to-day challenges in our lives?
3. What can you do to more fully prepare yourself and your family for life's challenges?
4. How are you encouraging your kids to be prepared for the next day's challenges (homework, practice, etc.)?
5. How are you preparing your children for life's emotional and spiritual challenges?

Passion: Live Like You Were Dying

Dear Hunter,

I love you, son. Anyone who has ever been with me for even a few minutes, or has ever set foot in our house, knows that we were passionate about loving you. I made some mistakes, Hunter. I made a lot of mistakes, and for those I have found forgiveness from God. I love the way you lived your eight years. I love the way you lived with passion.

Always,
Your dad

Matt Hamill has passion. He's here with me at football camp because a film company that I have a stake in is making a movie about his life. Matt was born hearing impaired, but has turned his passion for wrestling into a career as a top mixed martial arts fighter. He has a passion for training and competition that absolutely blows my mind.

It's not that I have a passion for film, really. For example, I couldn't tell you the difference between a "movie" and a "film." I watch movies. Other people watch films. I'm involved in a film company because I love being around people with passion.

And even though Matt is just hanging around, signing autographs, I can see his passion. He's got a fresh cut on his face from a recent fight, and the inside of his eye—you know the soft, sensitive part that you cry from—looks like it got ripped into. I've been around football a long time and have either had or seen most injuries, but this one is especially gross. Matt's picture is next to the word "tough" in the dictionary, right after my son, Hunter, of course.

When I was growing up, I admired Rocky Bleier's passion. Rocky was a running back for the Steelers—one of those guys about whom they always said he got by more on grit than talent. But he was pretty talented too. Rocky fought in the Vietnam War, defending our country, and when he spoke about that, or football, I sensed his passion. Rocky was injured in the war when he was struck by both an enemy bullet and some shrapnel when his platoon was attacked in a rice paddy. He was told he'd never play football again. When he was recovering in a hospital in Tokyo, he received a postcard from Steelers owner Art Rooney which read, "Rock, the team's not doing well, we need you." He was inspired to return to football—a process that took him a full two years. When he reported to his first camp, he was a gaunt 180 pounds and couldn't walk without a limp. He was waived from the team twice. Finally, in 1974 he stuck and would from that point on remain in the starting lineup. He played in the four Steeler Super Bowl victories and rushed for 1,000 yards in 1976 (along with teammate Franco Harris). Bleier played, and lived, with passion.

Bleier came to speak at a football banquet after my junior year in high school. He was my second-favorite Steeler, next to Terry Bradshaw. That night, at a Holiday Inn in Butler, Pennsylvania, was one of the greatest of my life. He spoke with passion about his experiences in Vietnam and the NFL. I was mesmerized. When I met him, I said, "I'm going to play for the Steelers someday." He said, "Jim, I was impressed by what I saw on the film tonight. You're quite an athlete. You're going to be somebody someday." I was flying about as high as I could fly at the time.

Passion and the Bickering Bills

I think all great leaders have it. My high school coach, Terry Henry, had it. Howard Schnellenberger, my coach at Miami, had it. So did Jack Pardee with the Houston Gamblers, and so did Marv Levy. And he needed all of it in 1990. We were starting to get a reputation around the league as a talented team with personal problems. We were called "The Bickering Bills." In 1989 I blamed tackle Howard Ballard for giving up the sack that separated my shoulder, and then Thurman Thomas got on my case, rightly. As a leader, I should have never publicly shamed my teammate. And we should have never done it in the media because by then every time a camera caught a heated exchange on the sideline—and every football team on the planet has these—they used it as proof that we were falling apart. Darryl Talley called us "the misfit toys from Christmas." We were living proof that to be successful a team has to have passion, but that passion has to be tempered by self-control.

You live and learn from mistakes in pro football and in life. Behind the scenes, Howard and I sat down, I apologized, and we talked it out. To succeed in sports, life, or business, you have to be able to communicate. And if you're going into battle with your teammates, you have to be able to trust them and know that they're going to have your back. We knew as a team that we had talent, but we couldn't continue to battle with each other. When you have a lot of egos on a team, sometimes there are too many chiefs and not enough Indians. We all have our moments, but it's what you do about it that counts.

As you think about raising your kids, are there areas in which your ego, and your desire to be right, gets in the way like it did with Howard and me? What are your passions in life, and how are you keeping them in perspective? The Bills in that time illustrated the importance of passion—we had guys like myself, Darryl, and Thurman who absolutely loved the game. But we were also an example of the need to control that passion.

We had won the AFC East the season before, but got crushed by the Dolphins, 30–7, in the second week of the 1990 season. We had five Pro Bowl players on our roster and the league's best defense, but couldn't get over the top. We had a lot of finger-pointing and backbiting in our locker room in 1989 and couldn't afford more of the same in 1990. But in Miami, our defensive end Bruce Smith openly questioned Marv Levy on the sidelines after he decided to take out most of the first unit offense (including me) when we were down 30–7. The fact of the matter is that we were like a big family, and families fight.

We played the Jets in the third week of the season, in the Meadowlands, on Monday night. The Jets opened the game with a five-minute drive that ended in a touchdown, and we were all kind of thinking, "Here we go again."

On our first series, after getting flagged twice for offensive pass interference, I hit Keith McKeller on a deep corner route, and then Kenneth Davis punched it in. It was important that we responded to adversity right away, with a score of our own. In a pregame interview I said there was no dissention on our team—there was still some rumblings, but we were definitely getting better. What we needed, more than anything, was some success.

One of the things I appreciated the most about Marv Levy was his leadership style. He wasn't a yeller and screamer. Marv would speak through war heroes by telling us different stories. He would introduce us to people who have achieved greatness and try to get you to visually put yourself in their shoes. When he spoke, he spoke volumes. And when he was mad, you knew who the general was. Marv idolized Winston Churchill because he grew up listening to his speeches on the radio during World War II. Some players think a generation gap is a bad thing, but with Marv it was a blessing. We just soaked up his knowledge and experience. As everyone knows by now, Marv was very intelligent—a Harvard grad (MA in English History). But he never insulted our intelligence... and never talked down to us. Well, mostly never. Sometimes in team meetings he'd throw out a big word... like "antediluvian" or something. And he'd always look at Thurman Thomas and say, "Thurman, look that up." It always broke the tension in the room.

Speaking of Thurman, he ripped off a huge run in the first quarter of the Jets game. He was a long holdout through the off-season and preseason and only had 22 yards rushing against the Dolphins, so this run was proof that his legs were back underneath him. The 60 yarder was the longest of his career. Later in the same drive he busted a 20 yarder on a little option look where I actually took a snap under center, reverse pivoted to freeze the defense, and then pitched to Thurman. It felt like high school. Thurman had almost 150 yards rushing before halftime. He would end up averaging about 12 yards per carry.

And in the second quarter, I hit backup tight end Butch Rolle in the end zone. In the two years previous, Butch had six catches, and they were all for touchdowns.

Cornelius Bennett forced a fumble in the fourth quarter, and a few plays later I hit Keith McKeller to make it 30–7, Buffalo. What a difference a week makes.

A week later we would welcome the Broncos to Rich Stadium. They had beaten us 28–14 the previous year and were always dangerous with John Elway and his cadre of receivers. Their star had fallen a little bit since the 1980s, but they could still do damage and we wanted to avenge last year's loss. Our defensive coordinator, Walt Corey, was committed to bringing pressure off the edges with Bruce Smith and Cornelius Bennett—and by season's end most people in the NFL would agree that we had the best pass-rushing tandem in pro football. Bruce was a beast early on in this game—bringing heat on Elway and making plays in the running game. He was a little underrated in terms of how solid he was against the run. Bruce was also an underrated leader in the sense that he didn't speak often on the field, but when he did, it got everybody fired up. Unfortunately, none of what he said on the field would be printable here.

What was unusual about this game is that their running game was going early. Bobby Humphrey—who incidentally had the best high-top fade in professional football, he looked like Kid 'N Play—led a seven-minute drive and jammed it down our throats from the one-yard line. It was rare to see our defense get worn out that way. What was also unusual was the first half I had. Denver's defensive coordinator Wade Phillips was putting a lot of defensive backs on the field and sitting back in zone coverage, which let their big safeties— Steve Atwater and Dennis Smith—read my eyes and make plays. Atwater was the size of an outside linebacker, but ran like a wide receiver. He picked me off late in the first half, and that led to Elway throwing a beautiful corner route to Vance Johnson at the same time that he was getting slammed to the turf by Talley. Elway was a tough guy, and I have nothing but respect for him, but we were doing our best to beat him. Their running back Steve Sewell scored a couple of plays later, and we were down by two touchdowns.

Bruce, who would be named the AFC's Defensive Player of the Year in 1990, got us a huge turnover in the third quarter, which gave us the ball on their ten-yard line. We only had ten yards to go, but on the first two plays after the turnover, it seemed like ten miles. I had about two weeks to throw on the first play, but because of the Broncos coverage, nobody was open and I had to wing it out of the back of the end zone. The next play was basically the same thing, except instead of throwing it away I took a coverage sack instead. We finally beat Atwater and all those DBs on the next play. I came to the line of scrimmage and saw all their defensive backs and checked to a direct snap to running back Don Smith, who took it into the end zone. Sometimes the best pass is the one you decide not to throw.

Our inconsistent play continued in the third quarter when I botched a handoff to Thurman. But as I was jogging off the field, I tapped him on the helmet just to let him know we were going to be alright and that I wasn't pissed. One of the important things about being a teammate/leader is letting people know you believe in them, no matter what. A few plays later Sammy Winder scored on a short run, on the exact same play that Steve Sewell scored on in the first half.

We were trailing 21–9 in the fourth quarter when our defense came to life. Elway had had a pretty pedestrian day, and our pressure started to get to him, resulting in bad throws, interceptions, and knocked-down passes. Cornelius Bennett ran a blocked kick back for a score, we got an INT returned for a touchdown, and ended up winning 29–28. We beat the Jets again, at home, in week 7, with 19 seconds left to play on a pass to Jamie Mueller.

In week 9 we rode a couple of Darryl Talley interceptions to a 42–0 route of the Cleveland Browns. It felt really good to take the Browns—especially after what happened in the playoffs the year before. Darryl was one of my best friends and was a great leader on our football team. He led our team in tackles in 1990 and was always underrated. He started calling himself Rodney, as in "Dangerfield," as in "gets no respect." We respected him in the locker room. The best thing about Darryl is that he was quick, strong, fast, and loved knocking the crap out of everything in his path. We had a lot of guys like that on our defense, but he was the ringleader. Marv once said that we got the best out of Bruce Smith because of Darryl, and I believe him.

Darryl called me "Heathcliff" because he said I was a cat

who thought I was a dog. Even though I was a quarterback, I would run around and dive and hammer people, and he thought I played like a linebacker. Truth be told, that's about the highest compliment anybody could give me.

It was misty and cold in week 15 when we played the Giants at the Meadowlands, in what would be a preview of our Super Bowl matchup. It was a classic, northeastern, cold-weather game for that era—sleet/freezing rain, wind, and a game played on Astroturf. It's the kind of day where you can see the icy water splash up whenever anybody hits the turf, which is extra motivation to stay off of it. We were leading the league in scoring, and they were leading the league in scoring defense, so something had to give. The Giants had a classic power team, led by Ottis Anderson who at the time was the number eight rusher in the history of the NFL—a very under-rated guy who we would see a lot more of in the Super Bowl. They had a stable of other big backs too—like Lewis Tillman and a rookie named Rodney Hampton out of Georgia—and would just send these guys at our defense in waves. It seemed like they didn't pass for the entire first drive. Parcells seemed to take sick pleasure in just showing teams how he could run on them. And he could, most of the time.

The Giants' opening drive seemed to take about an hour, and they called exactly one pass play. They went for it on a fourth and goal and punched it over on the ground.

We responded quickly though. Running the no-huddle, I hit Thurman on a flare pass, and he exploded up the sideline to put us in scoring position. One of Thurman's strengths was his patience—his ability to set up his blockers perfectly and wait for a play to develop. He got an amazing kick-out block on the cornerback from Will Wolford and then saw the crease and went for it. A couple of plays later I hit Andre Reed on a crossing route, and just like that we were tied up. Those two drives were a great example of how differently our two teams operated—New York was slow and methodical, while Buffalo could hurt you in a heartbeat.

Andre Reed is a great example of the fact that, leadership-wise, I'm a firm believer that not everybody should be treated the same. Getting in someone's face is not always the right way to lead. The person, ultimately, needs to respect you, believe in you, and follow you. For example, Andre was a little bit more sensitive. Like all great receivers, he felt that he was always open, and he always wanted the football. I blew up at him every once in a while, just to remind him that my job was to read defenses, not just throw it to one receiver. But the thing is, when I threw it to him I was always glad I did. To this day he's one of the most underrated players in NFL history and was especially good at breaking tackles in the open field after the catch.

Kent Hull, on the other hand, always saw eye-to-eye with me, and on the rare occasions he didn't, we would always just talk it out. Kent was a very smart player and a very capable leader himself. He made all of the calls at the line of scrimmage for our offensive line, and people always responded well to him. With Steve Tasker, he never said much, but people respected how hard he played the game. And Darryl Talley was our defensive leader—he was a vocal leader on the field and always knew where to put people to get them in position to make plays. Every defense needs a guy like that.

The Giants were lined up defensively with only two down

defensive linemen and five linebackers because more and more often we were spreading teams out with multiple receivers, rather than trying to run right at them with the power game. The Giants were trying to disguise coverages and come up with unique ways to bring pressure. In 1989 there were rumblings about my fundamentals being suspect—especially in the area of decision making. In 1990 I felt much more comfortable seeing and calling things at the line of scrimmage, and I think it was beginning to show. I was throwing off my back foot less, and I was developing much more poise and confidence. We had the most potent offense in football, and at the time I was the highest-rated quarterback in the NFL, completing around 64 percent of my passes, with 23 touchdowns against only 9 picks.

We won 17–15, but I felt a sharp pain in the side of my knee and went down on a routine pass play in the second quarter. I stepped into a throw, and one of my own guys, Will Wolford (who weighed more than 300 pounds), was driven back into my left knee, which was completely locked out. When I went down, and was writhing on the field in pain, a huge cheer went up from the Meadowlands crowd. Always classy. I was feeling the worst pain I had ever experienced. I just sat on the field and rocked and thought about losing a season that had so much promise.

I managed to walk to the sidelines slowly, and after a little while the pain subsided completely. I even told Kent Hull that I'd be back in the game soon. I did some deep knee bends on the sideline and really thought I'd be able to shake it off. Unfortunately I was dead wrong. My knee buckled on the sidelines, and House Ballard caught me before I hit the ground for good. I went back to the locker room on the back of a utility cart and Frank Reich did his usual great job, sticking with the K-Gun offense (which, by the way, was named after Keith McKeller and not me) and leading us to victory.

It goes without saying to anyone who played on those teams or even followed football in the early '90s, but Frank was the best backup quarterback in pro football. Being a backup quarterback is a unique job. Without a doubt, backups were always the best quarterbacks on their high school and college teams, and probably in their college conferences. These are star players who have to get used to just practicing every week, taking their reps, and "being ready." Frank was always ready, and whenever he got a chance to play he always won the respect of his teammates. Our guys truly believed in him, and it showed. Teddy Marchibroda would always say, "You're only one play away from being a starting quarterback, so you have to prepare yourself as a starter."

The doctors said it was sprained ligaments, and I had to watch the next week as Frank quarterbacked us to a victory over the Miami Dolphins to clinch our division. That win earned us a bye in the first week of the playoffs, and I used it to rest my knee. Resting my knee that week was the right thing to do, but let me tell you, standing on the sidelines and watching somebody else run your offense, lead your men, and do your job is one of the hardest things in the world to do. The NFL is a here-today-gone-tomorrow kind of league, and you never really feel completely secure because the best athletes in the world are competing for your job. I hated sitting out, at every level of football, but especially now, with a team that had so much potential.

Incidentally, just as an example of where my mind was at the time, while I was injured I asked a roomful of reporters, "What have I done wrong? I go to church every Sunday. I pray. God, I just don't know . . ." I was wallowing in self-pity about an injured knee, and I had no idea about the kind of journey that awaited me after retirement. God had other plans for me. Plans that were much bigger than football games.

We opened the playoffs at home, where we were 23 of our last 25, against Miami. It was a typical Buffalo day—about 33 degrees with rain changing to snow. Just how we liked it, especially against a warm-weather team. I had rested my knee at the end of the season against the Dolphins and Redskins. A lot of the writers and talking heads thought I shouldn't have played against Miami in the playoffs because I wasn't completely healthy. To be honest, there was no way I was missing that game. Mark Clayton, from the Dolphins, said he didn't understand how I could play at all because he had suffered a similar injury. I wore a huge, bulky knee brace and didn't move around as much, but like I said before, I was going to go. That was never a question. I knew my teammates were relying on me, and I wanted to get out and play. Especially since I knew the kind of beating my teammates took throughout the course of a season. Andre Reed went across the middle all the time and got the crap knocked out of him and just kept coming back for more. Kent Hull had bent fingers, shot knees, bad shoulders, and everything else. One of our offensive linemen, John Davis, could hardly walk.

Some of the writers were joking with Marv, who was 62

at the time, about whether he could beat me in a footrace now that my knee was banged up. Marv said he could have beaten me before the knee. There was probably some truth to that. Marv jogged like five miles every day. I was never known for my sensational open-field running...but I liked to run and could when I needed to.

We were a quick-starting team—we scored on most of our opening drives, and I think we'd scored on seven of our last ten. Thurman ripped off a fourteen-yard run, and then we went to the air. I hit Andre Reed on a post route, and he just exploded between the corner and the free safety, taking it to the end zone. The great ones all have an extra gear, and Andre definitely had it. I pumped my fist at the crowd when I came off the field after that throw because I knew I was completely back, and they knew it too.

Dan Marino was the heart and soul of that Dolphins team, but his star receivers—Mark Duper and Mark Clayton—were aging, and they never could really get their running game going. They would have trouble running against us because of our two Pro Bowl linebackers—Cornelius Bennett and Shane Conlan. Conlan was one of those tough, gritty, under-rated Penn State guys who was actually a much better athlete than he got credit for. Maybe I would have turned into Shane Conlan had I accepted that scholarship to play linebacker at Penn State! Our whole linebacking corps was great. We had another guy, named Ray Bentley out of Central Michigan, who had long, stringy hair and used to paint his face up like the rock star Alice Cooper, with black above and below his eyes and running down his cheeks. He was a real evil-looking character. Every team needs a few characters like Ray Bentley.

The Dolphins had a huge fullback named Tony Paige who was probably the best lead blocker in the NFL. He would give our linebackers all we could handle. One of my favorite things about the fans in Buffalo was the way they appreciated great defense. They cheered just as loudly for a tackle for loss in the first quarter as they did for a touchdown pass to win a game in the fourth quarter. They were passionate and they knew their football, and our defense completely fed off that.

Later in the first quarter I hit James Lofton on a go route, right up the right sideline. He beat Tim McKyer by a couple of steps and did an amazing job of finding the ball. McKyer, a cornerback, was famous for the amount of trash he talked both during the week and during ball games, but he said before the game that we were "wonderful competitors" and "remarkable human beings" and that he had "nothing but respect for the city of Buffalo." He also complained that Lofton was grabbing his face mask and pushing off...although he didn't need to on this play.

I was also getting an unbelievable amount of time to throw from my offensive line. They were having a great year, and as a result so was I. I had more than one hundred yards passing before the first quarter was over.

Nate Odomes got us the ball back when he picked off a Marino deflection. It started to snow midway through the first quarter, and later in the drive I got flushed from the pocket and decided to run. I picked up sixteen yards and fumbled...and luckily Kent Hull was there to fall on it and bail me out. But more importantly, the knee was feeling good. In fact, everybody started to feel comfortable earlier in the week when before practice our trainer accidentally taped my good knee and when he was halfway done, I realized he taped the wrong knee.

Once the snow started flying, we began to run the ball effectively. One of the things that Marv thought was a drawback to the no-huddle was the fact that it took us out of the running game...but I think Thurman was just way ahead of his time in terms of his ability to run and find holes out of a shotgun formation. We weren't a power team, but we were still very effective on the ground. People think it was all draws and delays out of the shotgun, but we actually ran the same kinds of stuff other teams did, except that Thurman was lined up beside me. We made a living on the ground running counter-gaps, which were the same plays the Redskins used out of more traditional, double-tights power formations.

Speaking of running, I ran a ton in this game. Miami was coming hard off the edges, trying to flush things inside, figuring that I wouldn't try to get outside the pocket. They were right. Instead, I stepped up and ran up the middle several times, which isn't ideal but hey, it's the playoffs and you do what you've gotta do. When you're in the heat of the moment and when you're playing with passion, you don't think about an injury or a taped knee. The fact of the matter was that by that point of the season everybody was banged up.

And speaking of doing what you've gotta do, Marv allowed us to go for it on a fourth and one in the second quarter, and Andre Reed—who was the king of getting open in those situations—got open and I hit him across the middle. James Lofton and Andre were absolutely carving up the Miami secondary, and I hit Lofton for a touchdown to end the drive.

Thurman added a five-yard touchdown run, and I added a 26-yard touchdown pass in the fourth quarter, to make the score 44–27 with less than ten minutes remaining. Marino would toss one more touchdown of his own, to make it 44–34, at the gun. I had connected on 19 of 29 passes for 339 yards and three touchdowns, compared to only one interception. And even with my knee heavily bandaged, I ran three times for 37 yards.

Cultivating Well-rounded Passions

If I were to only communicate my passion for football in this chapter, I'd be sorely understating things. I think well-rounded people cultivate many passions. Off the field I've always been passionate about my family and friends—which is why the Kelly house has always been an off-field destination for many of my teammates and their families.

I'm passionate about hunting for many of the same reasons I was passionate about football—it requires concentration, preparation, the right equipment, and a commitment to getting the job done. It's also been a great way to continue to be challenged alongside other people. There are few things I appreciate more than a perfect day of hunting—great times with great people in nature.

And finally, God, through Hunter, gave me a passion for helping to save kids' lives as well as doing whatever it takes to improve the quality of life for suffering children through Krabbe disease research and the Hunter's Hope Foundation, which I'll go into in greater detail later. I can honestly tell you that there's nothing like seeing a kid live a longer, fuller life because of some of the things we've been involved in with the foundation. It's a purpose in life that transcends throwing a football. It's a real passion that transcends time.

But God used my first passion—football—to get us here.

———

I really felt like the Bills had arrived, as a team, in the 1990 AFC championship game against the Raiders. We were undefeated at home that entire season and felt like we couldn't lose in Rich Stadium in front of our home fans. It wasn't too windy, so we felt like we could throw against them, but we also had to shut down their deep passing game, as they liked to air it out to Willie Gault. Rain, and eventually freezing rain, was in the forecast, and the cold temperatures gave the turf at Rich Stadium the consistency of green concrete. We felt like this played to our advantage against a team from Southern California.

My knee was really hurting me, but there was no way I was going to miss any time with it. By the end of the playoffs in the NFL, everybody is playing hurt. Nobody is at full strength. We started the game with two big plays by Thurman Thomas—I called a draw play up the middle on the first play, and then we hurried right back to the line of scrimmage and he ran a little angle route over the middle for another first down. Our pace was fast and furious, and we were the best conditioned team in the NFL. It was hard for defenses to keep up with us, in terms of getting the right personnel on the field, but it was also hard for them to keep up with us physically.

The beauty of calling plays in advance, or even calling plays quickly at the line of scrimmage, is that it forced the

Raiders to stay in their two-deep base defense while we were spreading out the field with four and five wides. And having a back as talented as Thurman allowed us to line him up in the slot and work him against linebackers, which is a matchup that I would take advantage of all day long. Their linebackers were walking around tired with their hands on their hips three plays into the game. Kudos to our offensive coordinator Ted Marchibroda, who never got enough credit, and Marv Levy for having the guts to let me be aggressive at the line of scrimmage. It was both of our jobs on the line.

Ted Marchibroda really taught me how to watch film as a professional quarterback, and he really taught me to communicate. I loved Ted because he was as excited as I was, and we had the same driven personalities. And he was open to suggestions. He ran a great meeting room with myself and Frank Reich—he knew exactly how to communicate with both of us.

Marv and Ted decided to let me call plays following the 1989 playoff loss to Cleveland. In that game we started running our two-minute drill exclusively and almost came back to win the game at the end. In the off-season, they decided to start the 1990 season that way, and it worked so well that we stuck with it. They were both putting their necks on the line by allowing me to call my own plays. I was the only NFL quarterback doing that in 1990, and if it crashed and burned, we were all going to crash and burn together.

On the third play we ran a post to Andre Reed and picked up another first down. Everything was working. The Raiders ended up calling a timeout just to regroup...like a basketball team trying to stave off an early game run.

They asked me before the game if it was the biggest game in my life, and I said, "Are you kidding? Of course it is." We were playing for a chance to go to Tampa and play in Super Bowl 25. I had dreamed of this my whole life...but the truth of the matter is that the biggest game of my life was whatever game I was playing in at the moment. They all mattered to me.

What's weird is that the Raiders stayed in their base defense after the timeout. They still had linebackers in the game, like Riki Ellison, who were geared to stop the run but who couldn't stay with our guys—like Thurman and tight end Keith McKeller—on crossing routes. Is should be noted that McKeller was Antonio Gates before Antonio Gates was. He was a college basketball player at Jacksonville State in Alabama who only played one year of college football, and came to us as a project. But he was the kind of height/weight/speed guy who was too good to pass up.

The Raiders had some great defensive linemen, like Howie Long, Bob Golic, and Scott Davis, but they were gassed trying to keep up with our pace. The speed at which we played the game was our way of neutralizing their pass rush.

On the last play of that first drive, I dropped the shotgun snap, and the ball was dribbling around on the turf for what seemed like forever. It's at those moments that your life really slows down. Even though it's cold and there are eighty thousand people screaming at you, and twenty-one other guys moving around violently, your whole life becomes centered around picking up the ball. I did pick it up and barely avoided being crushed by Raiders defensive end Greg Townsend. I moved to my right and found James Lofton drifting across the middle. Like all great veteran receivers, he had broken off his route and was just trying to be an outlet. I hit him with the pass, and he ran in standing up.

Just as an aside, I have to remind myself sometimes how amazing it was to be able to play with Andre Reed AND James Lofton. Most quarterbacks don't get to play with ONE Hall-of-Fame-caliber receiver in their careers, but I got to play with two—three if you count Thurman when he lined up in the slot or ran routes out of the backfield. The collection of talent that Bill Polian put together on that team was outrageous.

Lofton had already played with Green Bay and the Raiders and had never gotten this far. He was motivated to get to a Super Bowl and add that accomplishment to his already impressive résumé. The Raiders brought in an extra nickleback on the next series, but fortunately (for us), Lofton was playing out of his mind. Even though he was in his thirteenth season, he still had the speed to beat Raiders corner Lionel Washington one-on-one, and I hit him over his left shoulder on the second series. Two plays later Thurman broke one up the middle for a touchdown, and I knew the route was on.

The next time we got the ball—after a Darryl Talley interception for a touchdown and another great defensive series—the Raiders went to a three-man line and just dropped everybody else into coverage. I had all day to throw the football, and I even hit Steve Tasker—our special-teams stud—with a pass. It was only his third catch all season. He wore number 89, a receiver's number, but he was really like a hybrid strong-safety/special-teams maniac.

Of course, when they went to three down linemen, we started to hammer away at them with Thurman. Even though we were in a shotgun, he was so good at getting to top speed quickly it was as though we were running right at them. The beauty of this offense—much like Peyton Manning's today—is that it gave us the flexibility to get into the play we needed at the line of scrimmage, based on what the defense showed us. We could still do almost anything we wanted to in the running game, even though we were in a shotgun formation, because our offensive linemen were so versatile and athletic. We had some of the best pulling guards in football—guys like Jim Ritcher and John Davis.

I took a hard shot in the second quarter when, on the goal line, we tried to run a fake dive left, bootleg left, that didn't fool anyone on the Raiders defense. I never considered myself a "running quarterback," but I was an athlete. I felt like I was good enough to run, and I'd made a number of plays with my feet during the years. I can hear my center, Kent Hull, laughing right now.

Even our backup running back—Kenneth Davis, who was good enough to start for most NFL teams—scored three times (which tied an AFC championship record) behind crushing lead blocks from fullback Jamie Mueller. Jamie played at a tiny college in Kansas called Benedictine, and we used a third-round draft choice on him. I don't know how our personnel people found guys like that, but I'm glad they did. In the third quarter, on two plays back-to-back, he had pancake blocks on Raiders safety Mike Harden and cornerback Lionel Washington. Both guys looked like they'd been run over by a truck. If you watch the film, you can hear the fans going nuts when Jamie made his blocks. Only Buffalo has fans cool and savvy enough to go crazy for big blocks.

Darryl Talley picked up his second interception, in the fourth quarter, and it really started to sink in that we were going to Tampa to play in the Super Bowl. Our defense was dominant. We held star running back Marcus Allen to 26 yards on ten carries, and we'd picked Schroeder a total of five times, which led to scores and great field position for the offense. It's hard to lose when your defense is giving you the ball like that.

With just a minute or so to go on the clock, our offense was kneeling down to end the game and I was on the sidelines just noticing things. I looked across the field and saw the Raiders great defensive end, Howie Long, sitting on his helmet. All of the Raiders guys sat on their helmets. I also noticed that even though it was freezing outside, and the game was a blowout, not a single fan had left their seat. Cornelius Bennett was up on a heated sideline bench, dancing. Marv tipped his hat to the crowd, old school. It was very "Marv." The FCA guys all gathered in the middle of the field to pray. Jay Schroeder, even though he'd just had the worst day of his professional life, was in the middle. Jamie Mueller—he of the violent lead blocks—had a hand on Schroeder's shoulder. Win or lose, football is about relationships and about passion.

I picked up game balls and just started winging them into the stands as a way to thank our fans for their passion and loyalty. We were going to Tampa.

Dear Cam and Erin,

Through the years you've seen your dad pursue passions for many things—hunting, time with friends, good food, good wine, and of course, football. There were years

*that I thought I could never be as passionate about any-
thing, and anyone, as I was about football. That all
changed when you were born. I don't always do things perfectly, but I have a passion for the two of you, and I had a
passion for Hunter. Now I'm passionate about allowing
families who deal with Krabbe disease to find hope and
community and to love their children better. Thank you
for joining me in that! My prayer is that you'll find and
pursue God-honoring passions in your life and that you'll
pursue them with all you have.*

Always,
Dad

OFFENSIVE STRATEGIES

1. What are you passionate about? How do the things
   that you're pursuing reflect passion?
2. How do you make sure that you're passionate about
   the right things?
3. How do you recognize passion in other people?
   Why are we drawn to people who live their lives with
   passion?
4. How are you working to cultivate the right kinds of
   passion in your kids?

Perseverance: When It's Too Tough for Them, It's Just Right for Us

Dear Hunter,

I've talked to you about this on a few occasions, little buddy, and it's crazy to believe, but your dad was known for something that nobody in history has equaled—losing four Super Bowls in a row. It taught me a lot about perseverance. It taught me a lot about rising to fight again and coming back prepared each year. It taught me a lot about waking up every morning you were with us and deciding to thank God for the day and enjoy our life together. And YOU taught me a lot about perseverance as you battled something far greater than losing a game. Thank you for the example you set without saying a word and for the way you fought for life.

Always,
Your dad

The Power of Perseverance

> I'll just lie down and bleed a while, and then
> I'll rise and fight again.
>
> —Scottish poem

Whitney Houston had a great career, but if she'd done nothing at all except sing the national anthem before our Super Bowl with the Giants, she would still be a hero in my book. All through the Raiders game the previous week, the networks were breaking in to report on the Gulf War, and by the time the Super Bowl started, the United States was fully involved. It meant a whole lot more, as a player, to be standing there listening to this song that we had all heard thousands of times before in our careers.

This game was your classic "styles make fights" kind of game. Our offense was fast-paced and high-octane—I had thrown 24 touchdowns against only 9 picks, and our wideout James Lofton averaged more than 20 yards per catch that season. Thurman had almost 1,300 yards rushing and added another 600 or so in receiving, scoring 13 total touchdowns. The Giants, on the other hand, played power football. The Giants had a great defense that featured Lawrence Taylor and Pepper Johnson at linebacker, but their offense was just average. They were seventeenth in yards gained and thirteenth in points scored, but they were probably first in long, sustained drives that wore down defenses. They had an offensive line and a backfield that was built to mash. They lost their starting quarterback Phil Simms to a season-ending broken foot, but Jeff Hostetler who had only started a couple of games in seven seasons as a backup, filled in admirably, leading the Giants to two wins at the end of the season and leading them through the playoffs. Hostetler was a different kind of player. He was more mobile than Simms, which probably gave him more of a chance to survive against Cornelius Bennett and Bruce Smith.

Our return guy, Don Smith, was a college quarterback and came to us via the Tampa Bay Bucs. Smith gave us good field position to start the game, and even though I completed two crossing routes on that first series, they were short, and we didn't get the first down. This gave the Giants defense a ton of momentum, and they were sky-high.

The Giants ground down the field in typical Giants fashion, in a drive that ate up about seven minutes and gave them a 3–0 lead on a Matt Bahr field goal. We caught a break later that quarter on a 2nd and 8 situation in our own territory. The Giants were lined up with six defensive backs, but I decided to send Lofton long up the left sideline anyway. I underthrew the ball a little bit, and it was tipped by Giants defensive back Perry Williams. The Giants didn't want him singled up on Lofton, who of course had great speed and knew every trick in the book. That was exactly the matchup I wanted. Lofton was run out of bounds at the eight, right in front of all the Super Bowl photographers in their red vests. It was one of those quintessential Super Bowl moments—one of those plays you know will end up in a highlight film as soon as it happens. We couldn't punch the ball in from the 8, and Scott Norwood kicked a 23-yarder to tie the score at 3.

With thirty seconds or so left in the first quarter, I hit Andre Reed over the middle (where he lived all season), and he made the quintessential tough, Andre-Reed-type run after the catch. He got hit by Everson Walls down low and then Mark Collins up high, but nothing could hurt Andre. He popped right back up, and his toughness gave our offense a lift. Thurman made a tough run to close out the quarter and then a great catch and run over the middle to open the second. This game was really a tough-on-tough kind of situation. Our tough guys against their tough guys, all night long. And nobody was tougher than Thurman. He amazed me with the way he could take a beating and then pop right back up.

We ended that drive with a Don Smith touchdown run from the one-yard line. A former quarterback running behind a huge block from a fullback (Jamie Mueller) from Benedictine College. That touchdown was a great testament to the Bills front office and their ability to find talent. Incidentally, it was Don Smith's only carry in the game and the last carry of his NFL career. Even though he was primarily a blocker for us, Mueller was a two-time NAIA All-American in college. The Giants great linebacker Gary Reasons was usually money in these goal-line and short yardage situations, but he got absolutely crushed by Mueller on this scoring play.

Later in the quarter we had the Giants pinned deep in their own territory and Bruce Smith beat both their left tackle Jumbo Elliot and OJ Anderson to sack Hostetler in the end zone for a safety. Hostetler drifted a little to his left in his drop back and actually tripped over Anderson's right foot. Bruce, being the instinctive player he was, almost grabbed the ball and scored a touchdown. I couldn't believe he didn't fumble.

The Giants, running behind my old University of Miami teammate OJ Anderson, had a seven- or eight-minute drive to end the half. I can't overstate how much of a beast Anderson was on this drive. For a big guy, and an older back, he still had incredible burst and absolutely freight-trained our tough safety Mark Kelso on one run. Anderson wore these baggy, cotton game pants that kind of sagged down around his knees and looked like junior high practice pants. Honestly, he could have been wearing khakis and a golf shirt and he still would have gashed us that day.

When Anderson got tired, they hit us with their change of pace guy, Dave Meggett, who was kind of the anti-Anderson, stylistically. He was little and quick and had great short-area burst. With thirty seconds left in the half, we sent an all-out blitz, and Hostetler calmly found Steven Baker in the corner of the end zone with a perfectly placed ball. They called Steven Baker "The Touchdown Maker."

The Giants were famous for these long, ball-control drives, and the point was to keep our high-octane offense on the bench. And it worked. Between that long drive, a typically endless Super Bowl halftime, and then their first drive in the second half, it was probably an hour and a half before my offense got on the field again. It seemed like forever. A word on halftime: I hate halftime in general, but it's especially bad in the Super Bowl. You finally get into some kind of a flow and rhythm as a player, and then you have to go sit inside for a half hour.

The Giants started the third quarter with another one of their signature drives—a drive that had another one of those highlight-film plays in it. Anderson ran a counter trap behind guard Eric Roberts and then turned upfield where he ran through half our defense before delivering a WWE-style forearm right into the chops of Kelso. Speaking of tough on tough: they had a little receiver named Mark Ingram who was kind of their Andre Reed—their tough, over-the-middle guy. He made a catch on that drive on a 3rd and 13 where he broke tackles by Nate Odomes, Darryl Talley, and Kelso to pick up the first down. We died a little bit on that play.

OJ Anderson ran in from the one-yard line to cap the drive. He scored standing up. The drive ate up what was then a Super Bowl record nine minutes and twenty-nine seconds.

On the first play of the fourth quarter, Thurman exploded with a 31-yard burst to put us back up, 19–17. We were heavy favorites to win this game, and we hadn't expected to be in this kind of slugfest. Stylistically, it was exactly the kind of game the Giants wanted. Before our defense could catch its breath, the Giants were back on the field putting together another mammoth seven-minute drive. The drive ended with a Matt Bahr field goal, to put the Giants up 20–19.

The game came down to everything I'd ever dreamed about as a kid in East Brady—we had a little over two minutes to go and the ball on our own ten-yard line. We needed a drive to win the ball game. I started with a scramble to the 17. We hadn't converted a third down all game, but Thurman ripped off a long run to our 40 to give us a first down and keep the drive alive. After a few great runs from Thurman and a scramble by me, we got to their 29-yard line. The Giants hadn't decided to send much of a rush on the drive, opting instead to rush three linemen and drop everybody else back into coverage, allowing us to run and short pass our way down the field. I had all the confidence in the world in our kicker. When I came off the field, I could hear all the guys shouting "Good job, Jim!" We all stood there, holding hands, watching a little guy with a single bar on his face mask. I knew he would make it. It even looked good from the sidelines.

Wide right. You know the story. There's nothing quite as quiet as a losing locker room in football, and there's nothing quite as quiet as a losing locker room on the last day of the season. Looking around at all of the guys who tomorrow will be going their separate ways and who you've battled and bled with for months on end. Your awareness becomes heightened... you can hear pieces of tape being ripped off, you can hear dripping showers. It was especially quiet after the Super Bowl loss. Coach Levy simply walked to the center of the room and said, "There's not a loser in this locker room... so guys, hang in there." And that was it.

I felt bad for my teammates who had worked so hard, but I felt bad for my family, quite honestly—for my parents who had been there through everything and for my five brothers. I wanted this for all of them. I still want it.

Learning to Persevere as Parents

Losing in the Super Bowl really tested my ability to persevere. I've always said that football not only reveals character traits— like perseverance—but it develops them. The coming season would reveal our team's ability to persevere, but going through some of the things that football players go through also helps to build and develop perseverance.

It starts each year in the summer. There is nothing in sports quite as demanding as a football training camp. Even in high school. You're in the locker room early in the morning and everything is cold—your pads are cold, and your muscles are cold, sore, and tight from the previous day's practices. The bruises on your arms are fresh, and your body is relearning to take the kind of punishment it will endure during the course of the new season. Practices are long and hard, with lots of contact. They always culminate in conditioning— like wind sprints or gassers, and your body is so tired that even your teeth hurt. It's almost an out-of-body experience, pain-wise.

Between practices there are meetings and film sessions. Treatments for bumps and bruises. There is so much to remember...new plays...new terminology...even the combination on your locker. You learn to pull on a foreign-feeling helmet every day and get used to the weight of it on your neck.

Afternoon practice brings a whole new set of challenges. Your body is beaten and tired from the morning practice, but there is another two and a half hours of punishment ahead. Even worse than the physical challenge is the mental/emotional challenge of reconvincing yourself that it's worth it while your friends are taking their last trips to the beach or playing video games in an air-conditioned house. On top of that, your pads are wet with sweat from the morning practice. There's nothing grosser than putting on wet pads for the afternoon practice. I don't miss this. Not at all.

This process is repeated, day after day, for weeks. With ice bags, tape jobs, aspirin, fluids, calories, and hopefully lots of love and support from family to get a player through it. It happens every summer, in every town in America. And the beautiful thing about this process is that it teaches young men to persevere. It reveals to many of them that they're capable of doing hard things and surviving. And even thriving. In football, perseverance in any form is rewarded. There is perseverance through injuries, big and small. There is perseverance, at times, through the loss of a starting job. And the genius in these seemingly semimeaningless experiences is that they teach young men to persevere as older men.

Football reveals, and builds, our ability to persevere. Trials and challenges in life do the same things. As a young man, for me, it was losing four Super Bowls and coming back each year to try again. Since retirement, and as I've grown older, it has been challenges in my family and marriage. Things I couldn't have imagined persevering through.

God would challenge us through Hunter's life and death. He would challenge us through moments in our marriage when I didn't think we would make it. Sometimes I responded in the right ways, sometimes I didn't. But the more I reflect on it, the more I think losing those Super Bowls prepared me, uniquely, for what God knew I would go through later.

I think, as parents, that it's critical to model perseverance for our children. It's easy to think of trials as these sorts of cosmic injustices. Like God, or life, is doing us wrong. It's easy for us, as adults, to go into the "tank" emotionally or to turn to some unhealthy coping mechanisms. Our kids will learn to persevere as they see *us* learn to persevere.

It's equally important to shepherd our children through

their own trials. They are going to happen—broken friendships, challenges at school, and athletic mishaps. How do we respond to these things, as parents? Are we immediately blaming others? Or are we teaching our kids to classily persevere?

In life, perseverance happens when you are doing the right thing, and it's tough, and you start bleeding but you keep going anyway because it's the right thing to do and there will eventually be a finish line. Even if that finish line doesn't happen until heaven.

> *Dear Cam and Erin,*
>
> *You both faced so much trial as kids when you lost your brother. That event tested my faith more than anything else. I had dark days where perseverance was difficult, and I know you both dealt with it in your own ways as well. My hope is that you both learned to persevere through trials. If I've learned anything about life, it's that trials will come. I would never wish it on you, and my hope is always that we can grow in the Lord in other ways. But we've persevered together, as a family and individually as well. I'm proud of the way you persevered.*
>
> *Always,*
> *Your dad*

OFFENSIVE STRATEGIES

1. What are you being asked to persevere through in your life?

2. How has perseverance in the past helped you with current trials?

3. How are you helping your children to persevere through their own trials?

4. Are the trials in your childrens' lives developing or revealing their character?

Character: You Are Who You Hang With

Dear Hunter,

I was blessed in that the Lord put some amazing people in my life—people who made a permanent impact on me. Like some amazing coaches, some courageous teammates, my brothers, your beautiful mother, your amazing sisters, and you. There's nobody I'd rather hang with.

Always,
Your dad

My basement is like the basement you dream about when you're a kid. The walls are covered with jerseys from NFL greats like Terry Bradshaw and Joe Namath. In fact, there are so many jerseys in the basement that I don't have space to put them all up. I was down there the other day and noticed a Shaquille O'Neal Orlando Magic jersey I haven't been able to put up on my wall yet. No offense Shaq, I'm sure we'll get it hung up soon. With all the other greats to hang up, our new home doesn't have as much wall space in my man cave. The man cave isn't a priority anymore, like it was a few years back. But my buddies still love it, and we enjoy spending time there together.

There are pool tables and games, and at one end of the

basement is a bar, which has a huge mirror behind it that says "Kelly's Irish Pub." Beginning with the 1988 season, I started inviting all of my teammates and their families and friends to postgame parties in my basement, figuring it was safer and better for us to be together out of the public eye than to risk hitting the town and getting in trouble. Plus it was a great way for us to get to know each other and bond as a team.

The basement is quiet now, as it is most days, but after games it was full to bursting. Depending on how beat-up I was after the game, I would arrive and tend bar for a while until the players got there and would always make sure that food and drink were plentiful. My Aunt Toni from Pennsylvania had her secret spaghetti sauce and meatballs ready for the team. Man, I miss her sauce. And, thanks to the Certo Brothers, the cold refreshments were plentiful. There was always a challenge tournament going on at the pool table and a tape of the day's game was always playing on a big-screen television. Again, when people retire and say they miss things, these are the things they miss. I miss the activity in the basement. I miss the cast of characters and their families. And after it's over you're always sort of trying to recreate the mood of those evenings, but it's never really the same. There's no better feeling than coming home from battle and basking in it with your teammates and my five brothers. That's why there's no game like football, and there's nothing like being a player.

Finding a Woman of Character

It was at one of these parties, after a preseason game in 1991, that I met Jill. Here's what you have to understand about those parties, and about Buffalo: Buffalo, as we've discussed earlier, is basically a small town, so word (about everything) gets around. In Manhattan or LA, there are probably dozens of postgame parties at all kinds of swanky clubs. In Buffalo, my parties were the biggest show in town, and they were invite-only. Invitations were coveted, and we had this guy named Big Ed, who went about five-hundred pounds, guarding the door with the invite list.

Jill was a twenty-one-year-old, fresh out of college and living at her parents' house when she showed up with a friend of a friend that night.

Not surprisingly, she was intimidated. I mean, who wouldn't be in a loud, packed, strange house full of famous people and their semiglamorous friends? And quite frankly, I had set it up that way—"that way" being a little on the impressive/intimidating side. The walls in my hallways were lined with pictures of me with famous people and me with lots of beautiful women. Truth be told, I had semicultivated the image of the celebrity party animal/bachelor. Not to a Joe Namath degree, but probably closer to Namath than Bart Starr (or anyone else famous for clean living). I worked hard, but I played hard too. But, that was then, and much has changed since those days.

Luckily Jill saw through my carefully crafted public image, but it took a little bit of work on my part. We talked that night, but only a little. I got a chance to tell her that she had "the most beautiful green eyes" (she did). I asked for her number, and she declined. What I did next might be considered stalking—I found out where she worked and called her there. If Jill hadn't liked me, it probably *would* have been a little stalkerish. As it turns out, she agreed to go out with me, and I offered to send a limo to her folks' house to pick her up, which in retrospect is more than a little ridiculous, but at the time I thought it was a completely sensible move for Jim Kelly, Buffalo Bills quarterback. Cooler heads (Jill's) prevailed, and we agreed to meet at my house for the first date.

It was an adjustment for Jill to date somebody like me. She was constantly vying for my attention with the media, the public, and the Bills. It's not easy to date a professional athlete. But she had an abundant supply of patience, and we dated for three years (some of it long distance) before she moved in with me for good in 1994. This set about a wild ride of events that got us to where we are today. But I'm getting ahead of myself.

Let me explain something: at the time I was a leader of *men*. There's a certain way that football players communicate, and it's not elaborately or deeply. Football people are generally pretty short-winded, abrupt, and to the point. That's how I talked, and how I still talk to a certain degree. Intimate communication with a woman that involved real listening and the mutual sharing of feelings was kind of new territory for me.

This was put to the test for the first time when Jill told me she was pregnant with our daughter Erin. I had just returned from a long day of practice and films, and Jill sat me down in our bedroom and told me. I was afraid, but I brought her into my arms and told her everything was going to be okay.

I asked Jill to marry me on November 2, 1994, at Ilio DiPaolo's Italian bistro in my favorite private room. I knew Jill's life was changing. She was no longer herself—in a way, she was "Jim Kelly's girlfriend." I understood that, partially, at the time, but I don't think there was any way I could completely understand how that shift in identity would impact her. She was a smart, capable, beautiful, college-educated woman, but in a way her life was stuck in a perpetually high-schoolish cycle of pep rallies, tailgates, games, and postgame parties. She was kind of an adult cheerleader, for better or worse (contrary to popular belief, she was never actually a Bills cheerleader—called, ironically, the Buffalo Jills). Our life at this point was kind of a blur of family tailgates and Bills games. My folks and Jill's were disappointed that we lived together before we got married, but Jill received St. Alice's all-important blessing of approval and was assimilated into the Kelly clan.

Thank God, Jill said yes. Our wedding was a traditional Catholic ceremony, complete with big, beautiful church (St. Christopher's outside Buffalo), Father Oriole from my hometown, and Monsignor Francis Weldgen (a Bills chaplain) who said, "Buffalo has been waiting a long time for two things—to win a Super Bowl and for Jim Kelly to get married!" These kind of "bachelor" jokes make for great newspaper copy and lots of laughs, but I'm not sure they did anything to ease Jill's nerves.

Her dress actually landed her on *People* magazine's list of the ten best wedding dresses of 1997, along with the late JFK Jr.'s wife and Christie Brinkley. She was amazing, and I actually choked up while I was saying my vows. Not being one to really wear my emotions on my sleeve, this surprised everybody.

Our marriage was filled with ups and downs from the start. Jill's heart was hurting and breaking as I traveled often and she was left at home to sift through the remnants of my bachelorhood—all of the pictures and proof of my experiences with other women. This is something that should have been taken care of well before we were married, and it's also living proof that the things that you do before marriage (and who you hang with "that" way) can and will have a profound impact on the marriage you end up in. It has taken many years and lots of help (and will take more of both, I know) to heal some of those wounds.

Soon after we were married, I retired from the Buffalo Bills (more on that later) and Jill became pregnant with our son.

Hanging with Great Teammates

I was riding around in the truck the other day with my daughter, Erin. A story came on the radio that they were doing a twentieth anniversary article in *USA Today* on our four Super Bowl runs. Initially that kind of thing always freaks me out a little because the theme is always something like: what a shame that the Bills got there four times in a row (four times!) and LOST. I actually hate writing that word, and I certainly hate reading it. That's part of being an athlete and a competitor. I'd pretty much rather not think about any of those nights, which is why I've never watched films of those games. Of course, this gets tricky every year when I go down to the Super Bowl to hit up radio row and it's the first thing everybody wants to talk about. You get conditioned to give the same semicanned, semisincere answers about giving your best and coming up short and all of that. But I'm here to tell you that it (losing) still sucks.

But the older I get, the more I see articles like that and think about the guys I played with. The guys I hung with—the guys I respect. When we were making our Super Bowl runs, the radio stations here would change the words to popular songs so that they were about players from our teams. They had one that was about my pass to Andre Reed, and I played it recently for Erin. It's fun to share this stuff with her, and it's fun to think about my old teammates and friends. I promised Erin that one of these days I'd sit down and watch one of those games with her.

Regardless of whether or not that happens (though now it *has* to because it's in print), I'm pretty sure it won't be our loss to the Redskins in Super Bowl XXVI. I forced the ball a lot in that game and was something like 1 for 8 on third-down conversions. Coming into the game, we had led the NFL in total yards and were second only to the Redskins in scoring. We broke team records for total yards (6,252), net passing yards (3,871), completions (332), first downs (360), touchdowns (58), and touchdown passes (39).

Thurman and I had had the best seasons of our careers that year. He rushed for more than 1,400 yards and scored 12 TD's on the way to being named the NFL Offensive Player of the Year as well as the NFL Most Valuable Player. Even our backup running back, Kenneth Davis, rushed for more than 600 yards and scored 5 TD's.

I completed 64.1 percent of my passes for 3,844 yards and a league leading 33 touchdowns, with only 17 interceptions. We were hitting on all cylinders, and even though this Super Bowl was only the second one in league history to be played in a cold-weather climate (Minneapolis, Minnesota), we were still happy to be there. At least the game would be indoors. And we were confident even though our offense had been less than impressive in the AFC championship game against Denver. Thurman had been held to just 73 yards on 26 carries, and I threw for only 117 yards with two picks. Our offense didn't score a touchdown. We were surprised, but it didn't hurt our confidence going into the game. In fact, in my opinion we had our best week of practice that I'd ever experienced as a Bill. Even though the Redskins had a powerful offense, led by their offensive line "The Hogs" and their Hall of Fame receiver Art Monk, we expected to win. We always expected to win.

The Super Bowl has become such a spectacle that each telecast feels it has to outdo the previous season's somehow. The telecast for Super Bowl XXVI began with a broadcast from the space shuttle with some astronauts floating around in the air talking about the game. Nothing says football like astronauts floating around in the air. I guess they want to give the impression that even on the moon somebody cares about the Bills and the Redskins.

I was also kind of tweaked that they tried to interview me on the field during warm-ups before the biggest game of my life. I consider myself a laid-back, down-to-earth kind of guy, and I always liked talking to the media...but not minutes before the Super Bowl. That's just a little crazy. It blows my mind that now they "interview" each coach, on the field, right before the kickoff of almost every game. These are the kinds of hard-hitting journalistic interviews where the coach gets a microphone stuck in his face and then says something super insightful like, "We're going to do our best out there today."

That was just one example of how things were a little "off" for the Buffalo Bills. Another was the fact that Thurman couldn't find his helmet for the first two plays of the game. An NFL sideline is a flurry of activity, so it would be easy to sit your helmet down in one place and have another player move it or grab it, thinking it was theirs. At any rate, Kenny Davis started the game and gained a yard. On the second play I tried to call the play at the line of scrimmage—it was deafeningly loud in the Metrodome—and Kenny didn't hear me. He went right, and I went left for four yards before being crushed by Wilber Marshall. On third down the Redskins were on top of me, and I was sacked by defensive end Jumpy Geathers. I got up limping a little bit, but was clapping my hands and trying to let my teammates know I was okay. The truth is, none of us were really okay. That series was indicative of things to come.

The Redskins moved the ball at will. It seemed like every time I looked up, Mark Rypien was hitting Art Monk on a deep out route—he had five catches for 81 yards on the drive.

And to make matters worse, we lost our starting inside linebacker, Shane Conlan, for the rest of the game to a knee injury.

We figured the Redskins would blitz a lot because of the success that Denver had bringing pressure the week before in the AFC championship. Our blitz pickup was working all week in practice, but in the game I was getting shelled. The first play of our second offensive drive, with a rush in my face, I overthrew our receiver over the middle and was picked off by Redskins safety Brad Edwards.

I tried to force the ball deep to James Lofton in the second quarter and was picked by Redskins Hall of Fame corner

Darrell Green. I was desperate to get our offense going and was trying to do too much. The Redskins had a great secondary, led by Green and Martin Mayhew, who is now the Detroit Lions general manager. They lined up in a nickel defense (with an extra cornerback) with Alvoid Mays and Mayhew on the corners and Green in the slot on our best receiver, Andre Reed.

By the end of the first half, we were down 17–0 and I'd been sacked three times and thrown two picks. We showed some signs of life before halftime, driving to the Redskins' 28. I threw to Andre Reed, who thought he'd been interfered with. He slammed his helmet to the artificial turf and drew a fifteen-yard penalty, which pushed us out of field-goal range. We were unraveling as a group.

All told, I was sacked five times, hurried thirteen times, knocked down ten times, had two batted balls and four picks. My four interceptions in the game tied a Super Bowl record, which would eventually be broken, thank God.

By the middle of the fourth quarter they had already put the World Champions T-shirt and hats in front of each Redskins player's locker. The show must go on. By that point, we were just trying to make it respectable. On a scramble and slide in the fourth quarter I was hit by Mayhew on the way down, driving my left shoulder and head off the turf. That's when the lights were temporarily turned off. I was swearing at the trainers and refusing to leave the game. I wasn't all there, to say the least, but I knew I wanted to finish this thing out, even with as bad as it was going.

I threw a touchdown pass in the fourth quarter to my friend Pete Metzelaars and in the process had my brains scrambled again by defensive end Charles Mann. I don't remember much of what happened afterward, and I don't want to.

I vaguely remember getting dressed, and I knew where I was. I knew we'd lost, 37–24. But I didn't know what to do next. I knew my family was gathered at a hotel in Minneapolis, waiting for me for a postgame party that would feel more like an Irish wake. Our media director, Scott Berchtold, graciously spent half the evening going through the phone book calling all of the Holiday Inns in the Minneapolis area looking for my family. I had missed a television appearance after the game and subsequently missed the limo that was supposed to drive me to the hotel. My brain was only semifunctional.

When I finally got to the party and walked through the doors with my brother, I received a standing ovation from the hundred and fifty family and friends in attendance. I was touched. You are who you hang with.

Show Me Your Friends, and I'll Show You Your Future

NFL Hall of Famer Lem Barney, who was a great cornerback for many years with the Detroit Lions, once said, "Show me your friends, and I'll show you your future." Think about it. Your friends are your future. If you hang with the wrong people and they get you in trouble, you'll have no future. My dad, when I was a kid, always used to say, "Don't hang out with this kid or that kid." And you know what happened? Those kids always got in trouble. It's important that parents take a very hands-on role in whom their kids are spending time with.

Kids have it so much harder these days because of all the media outlets and the nonstop attention on celebrities. I remember reading a story recently about a thirteen-year-old kid signing for a football scholarship with the University of Tennessee. Thirteen years old! I was shocked.

That kid has so much life, and so much football ahead of him, and so many decisions to make, before he even steps onto the field in a college uniform. If he hangs with the wrong people, he'll take five steps backward. And as he begins to get into his junior and senior year in high school, when those pivotal decisions about drugs and alcohol are made, he will be made or broken by who he hangs with. Every young athlete is smart enough to know the difference between right and wrong.

I'm so fortunate to have been able to "hang" with some truly great people throughout my career. I honored many of them in my Hall of Fame speech:

My oldest brother, Pat, he taught me about hard work and has always provided me with wisdom and advice. Pat has written me letters ever since my college days. He congratulated me in times of victory and inspired me in times of defeat. He has always been the real field general amongst the Kelly brothers.

My brother Ed. Ed was the original quarterback of the family. Quiet and smart and something he has never known—he's a part of the reason I chose to be a quarterback.

I can always count on my brother Ray. He was always my honest critic. He always told it the way it was. Never sugarcoating anything. Thanks, Ray. I appreciate your straightforward comments more than you will ever know.

My twin brothers, younger brothers, Danny and Kevin. They have physically been with me every step of the way. From my college days at the University of Miami, to Houston and to Buffalo, where they both live today. Danny has been my most trusted confidant. The brother that I spend the most time with. To this day, I trust no one like my brother Danny. Then there's the youngest of the twins, Kevin. He is without doubt my biggest fan. After signing autographs for my brother Kevin for years and years, I finally asked him, "Kevin, who are all these autographs for?" He turned, looked and smiled, and said, "They're for me, bro, c'mon!"

God gave me exactly what I needed in my brothers. He gave me an encourager in Pat. For a bunch of guys who don't share their feelings, Pat always knew what to say and how to say it. He gave me a challenger in Ray and a quiet leader in Ed. He gave me best friends and confidants in Danny and Kevin. I'm so thankful and blessed.

Well, I learned the importance of an extended family as early as midget football where men like Art Delano, Gary Faust, Jim Martin, and Jimmy King, they were more than coaches. They gave me the guidance that went well beyond the football field, and for that I thank you, men.

Then there was my high school coach, Terry Henry from East Brady. He was a jack of all trades. He was our trainer, equipment manager, teacher, counselor, and father all rolled up in one. Not only for myself and for my brothers, but my teammates that are here today—Jimmy Hiles, Kevin Morrow, Paul Debacco, Danny Bigley, and many more. And to Terry, the fact that you remain so close to my family, to this day, speaks volumes. You will always be a key ingredient to why I made it as far as I did. I love you, Terry.

I mentioned Terry and Art earlier in the book, and I can't say enough about what Terry meant to me and the impact he had as a coach and a friend, even though I had a great support system already in place, in my family.

Coach Howard Schnellenberger's arrival to the University of Miami was a godsend to me. He was my father away from home. He was a drill sergeant. A hard-nosed coach. Something that every high school athlete needs, especially me. And with him came Earl Morrall, who taught me the ropes of how to prepare as a quarterback. And after injuring my shoulder my senior year at Miami, I was told that I would never play football again. But our trainer, Mike O'Shea, and my best friend and college roommate, Mark Rush, had different thoughts. They worked through countless hours of rehab with me to get me healthy enough to fulfill my dream of playing professional football.

Thanks, guys. And especially you, roomie, for pushing me to the limit every single day.

To Art Kehoe, Don Bailey, Tony Fitzpatrick, and my other college roommates Clem Barbarino and Greg Zappala, thanks for being much more than just Hurricane teammates.

And shortly after college, I joined the USFL's Houston Gamblers as a quarterback and then I left as a passer. Head coach Jack Pardee gave us direction. Mouse Davis, June Jones, and John Jenkins taught me the art of the passing game. Passing was never so much fun.

And then I made the greatest decision of my life—I became a Buffalo Bill. I can't think of a better owner to play for than Ralph Wilson, and his place in this Hall is waiting. He guaranteed me that he would provide the weapons for the Bills to be a Super Bowl team, and boy did he ever. Future Hall of Famers, Thurman Thomas...I don't know where I would have been without No. 34 behind me. Bruce Smith: the greatest defensive lineman to play; sorry, Deacon. I always thank God every day that Bruce was on my team.

Andre Reed: 12 plus 83 equals 664 receptions and 65 touchdowns. What more can I say, he is truly the best. James Lofton, the best long-ball threat in the game. And the greatest special-teams player ever, Steve Tasker.

Not to mention Darryl Talley, Jimmy Ritcher, Will Wolford, Pete Metzelaars, Don Beebe—another great long-ball threat, we thought we had to throw that one in there, Don—Kenny Davis, and of course, my personal coach in a jersey, there ain't no way I'd be standing here today without this man, my friend, my good buddy, Frank Reich.

And two guys that I played with at the end of my career, Alex Van Pelt and Ruben Brown. And the real reason that the no-huddle thrived the way it did, my center, my friend, and our great leader, Kent Hull. I love you, bro.

It occurs to me just how comprehensive this list is and how it contains family members at one level, friends at another, and coaches/authority figures at yet another. All of those groups combine, in a special way, to help shape a life.

Together, with my wife Jill, my daughters, and Hunter, they were the greatest teammates anyone could ask for.

Dear Cam and Erin,

Who you hang with is so critically important. Maybe more than any other chapter in this book, this is the one I really hope you read and internalize. Your friends have such an influence over the things that you do in life—big decisions and small. Make sure the people you hang with are people of high character. Make sure they're trustworthy and that they have your best interests at heart. Show me your friends, and I'll show you your future.

Love,
Dad

OFFENSIVE STRATEGIES

1. Are you intentional about the people you choose to spend time with?
2. What kind of example are you setting for your children, when they see the people in your life? Are the people you're hanging with a positive reflection of you?
3. Are you intentionally involved in your children's friendships?
4. What are some tangible ways to direct your children to positive friendships?

Responsibility: It Is What It Is (But Not Really)

Dear Hunter,

Life is full of responsibility. A lot of people think that because you're on television every Sunday, throwing touchdowns, that you somehow have less responsibility and less to worry about. That couldn't be further from the truth. Anytime we love people and let people into our lives, it comes with responsibility. Being your dad was the biggest responsibility I've ever undertaken—bigger than any football game or speech or business deal. And it was a privilege. The Lord is still teaching me through it.

Always,
Your dad

I have this plaque on my desk at the office that says, "It is what it is." What this is, on one hand, is one of the most overused clichés in sports. It's what an athlete or a coach says when they can't think of something more clever or appropriate to say. But it's also, I think, a way of accepting responsibility and moving on. It's a way to say, "I see the situation, I see my place in the situation, and I know my responsibility."

Living in Buffalo is basically great. Let me explain it in

simple terms: I really love this town, and Jill and I have decided to spend the rest of our lives here when we could've lived pretty much anywhere. And let's face it, almost everybody in this town who wants my autograph probably already has it. Still, being Jim Kelly in Buffalo comes with a fair share of responsibility.

Basically, I'm not allowed to have a bad day in public. When I walk out the front door in the morning, I'm not only representing the Kelly name, but I'm also kind of representing all of the accumulated years of history that I have in Buffalo and all of those guys that I played with, my family, and the Hunter's Hope Foundation. The thing is, the one autograph I *don't* sign is the one that will reflect on five thousand other people when that person goes home and tells their friends that Jim Kelly is a jerk—and those friends turn around and tell their friends.

As much as I love people and love fans, that's why my house is semisecluded and the lodge is truly secluded. I like to walk in the woods with my dogs. I like to grab a fishing pole and go down to the pond behind the lodge.

A disclaimer: I don't want this to be your typical "it's so hard to be famous" kind of chapter. Fame, just like anonymity, has its ups and downs and comes with its own unique challenges and responsibilities. It also comes with all kinds of thrills and perks for which I am eternally thankful. Those same fans who ask for autographs are the fans who, year after year, buy season tickets and jerseys and keep the NFL machine rolling. It's an interesting relationship. Fans and athletes will always need each other.

A lot of people think that when they approach an athlete, it automatically entitles them to a conversation. In a perfect world I'd be able to have a long conversation with everyone I meet, but the fact of the matter is that sometimes it's just not feasible. So if you're reading this and you've ever felt short-changed by me in a conversation, please accept my apology. It's not you, it's me.

There are also contexts—like a dinner out with Jill or my family—where it's hard to want to sign five or six autographs. It's complicated because sometimes it's actually *easier* to sign the autographs and shoot the breeze with a fan than it is to face the responsibility of having a family. This is why so many celebrities are sort of semipermanent road warriors. Because as long as you're on the banquet circuit where people think you're special and want to pat you on the back, you never have to face the fact that you're a real person with real problems and real responsibility. Rock stars talk about the "buzz" of being on the road, and this is what they're talking about. As long as you're flying from city to city, losing yourself in "activity," you never have to face the facts. I lived this way for a long time, and it's no way to live and have a family.

As a quarterback, you have a responsibility as the leader of the locker room and the leader on the field. Sometimes that means publicly admitting that you were wrong and accepting responsibility in a given situation. Right before Super Bowl XXVI, when the media was talking about how I called my own plays, our wide receiver James Lofton said, "In order to do that, you have to have big shoulders. Jim Kelly has big shoulders."

Responsibility Tested

I remember a time in 1989 when those shoulders were put to the test. We were slumping as a team, and for the first time really in my life as a quarterback, I was having a crisis of confidence. Our team was in the middle of a three-game losing streak. Our offense wasn't scoring a lot of points, and I was forcing the ball and creating turnovers. I leaned on my family, as always, to provide support. My dad said, "Every quarterback goes through some hard times, and you're no exception. But no matter what happens, you'll always have the support of your family. We're not going to let you go through this alone."

I did a couple of things in response to the slump. One, I decided to quit talking to the media for the rest of the season because all they wanted to talk about was the supposed bickering that was happening in our locker room. Two, we called a players-only meeting to clear the air, in which I took some responsibility for our underachievement. "We as an offense haven't been pulling our load, and I'm part of the reason for that," I said. "During the course of a season, the defense is going to have to come up with some big plays and win some games and the offense is going to have to do the same. We're all going to have to share in it. Don't worry about what the other guy does on this team. If everybody concentrates on their own assignments and what they're supposed to do, we'll be all right."

We just needed a reminder that each player had to focus on *his* responsibilities and not everyone else's.

One of the semiunfortunate realities of life in the NFL is

that sometimes you do your communicating through the media. The fact of the matter is that we're fallible people who make mistakes. Sometimes we wear our emotions on our sleeve. We were called The Bickering Bills, and sometimes we earned that nickname. NFL teams are comprised of a lot of people from very diverse backgrounds—different ethnicities, religions, musical preferences, and personalities. This can cause problems. I'd love to tell you that it was always bonding and best friendship in our locker room, but that wouldn't be true.

Responsibility in Adversity

In 1990 we were playing the Colts in Indianapolis at the Hoosier Dome. We were 3-1 and had built some momentum. In the third quarter I threw a 16-yard touchdown pass to Andre, but after I released the ball I was lifted off the ground and slammed to the turf by Jon Hand, the Colts' three-hundred-pound defensive end. I landed right on my shoulder, and it felt exactly like it did when I separated the shoulder in college against Virginia Tech. It was a sickening, pit-of-the-stomach kind of pain.

The docs knew it was serious immediately because I didn't get up. As a quarterback in the NFL, part of your job description is to get up after you get slammed to the turf. I took pride in popping right back up after each hit to show my teammates that I was still ready to battle. When the trainers got to me on the field, they asked me how much it hurt, and I said "Big-time."

Laying on the ground, I asked the question, "Why me?"

which is something I asked a lot when things went badly. I had this false understanding that if I was a "good person" and worked hard that nothing bad should ever happen to me. At the time I had no idea how screwed up this mind-set was. I would learn, later in life. What's funny is that I never asked "Why me?" when things were going great and I was winning, signing huge contracts, and having fun.

Anyway. Luckily for me there were no torn ligaments in the shoulder, and in a few weeks I would live to fight, and throw, again. But at a press conference later that week I said something that would plague me for the rest of the season. With my arm wrapped up in a sling, I mentioned that our tackle, Howard Ballard, missed the block that allowed Hand to crush me in the backfield. But I didn't stop there. I said the following to the reporters: "It should have never happened. Hand should have been blocked. Watching film, I don't know what Howard was thinking. It seemed like he was looking outside to see if a guy blitzed or something...and not at the guy over him." Geez. I also made reference to the line being solid in every place except one. Wow, great leadership, Jim (sarcasm). If I could have any public statement in my career "back," it would be that one. House was a good friend and the guy I always walked to the field with before games. He was my bodyguard, in every sense of the word.

Of course the media took that and ran with it. And in my first book I kind of blamed the media for blowing it out of proportion, but the fact of the matter is that I had given them lots of material to run with. For the first time in my career, it was cool to bash Jim Kelly. All of a sudden people were assuming that I had all of these privileges that other players didn't and that because of it I felt that I could say whatever I wanted. In some media outlets, the situation even downward spiraled into a racial issue.

I learned that many people resented the attention that was poured on me back in 1986 when I signed with the Bills. They were looking for an opportunity to knock me off my perch. And it taught me a huge lesson in responsibility. I started to become more responsible with my words because I knew that everything I said could and would, potentially, be used against me. I learned that there were a lot of people in Buffalo who loved Jim Kelly, but that there were also a lot of people who didn't.

Most importantly though, I had to talk with House privately and make things right, which I did. Those are hard conversations to have—the ones where you have to take responsibility and admit you're wrong—but I'm convinced that to a certain degree those are the conversations that determine who we are and shape the course of our lives.

Responsibility in Tragedy

But maybe more than any other time in life, the reality of responsibility hit me when we learned Hunter's diagnosis. When Hunter was born, all of his newborn tests checked out, and he appeared to us and to all the world as healthy and perfect. But by Hunter's third and fourth month, he was showing some serious physical abnormalities. He hadn't achieved any developmental milestones. His body was stiffening and becoming rigid, and he was having trouble swallowing. He even had some mild seizures. Our pediatrician referred us to a neurologist who ordered some blood tests. I knew something was wrong when she asked us to a consultation at her office. If it had been fine, she would have said so over the phone.

Jill and I were silent as we drove into the city. My brother Danny was waiting for us at Children's Hospital, where Dr. Duffner, the neurologist, and our pediatrician were waiting for us. I could tell by their demeanor and their expressions that the news wasn't good. The room was drab and window-less. At that point we weren't Jim and Jill Kelly, superstar quar-terback and beautiful wife, we were just another family about to have its world rocked. I'll never forget anything about it. How the room looked. How I felt.

"Your son has been diagnosed with a fatal genetic disease called Krabbe leukodystrophy. There is no treatment for this disease and no cure. The average life expectancy for babies diagnosed with infantile Krabbe is fourteen months. Hunter will probably not live to see his second birthday."

We learned that there was no additional treatment avail-able because nobody in the medical field was working on Krabbe's. "He'll need to get a feeding tube as soon as possible in order to eat, if that's what you choose to do."

I didn't cry in the consultation room, mostly trying to stay strong for Jill, but also because I was numb and shocked. I stayed quiet on the ride home as well. My first thoughts were that there was no history of disease in my family or Jill's, so where did this come from? I wanted to do anything...but for the first time in my life I didn't have any idea what to do, even though I was convinced that we shouldn't ever give up. We're Kellys; we don't give up.

At home Jill sobbed on the couch with Hunter, who

besides all the crying seemed healthy to me. I couldn't believe it. We would have to tell Erin, but how? I felt the weight of the world on my shoulders.

I responded, sadly, by running. By staying on the move. I was working as a color analyst for NBC (and later ESPN) at the time, and the schedule left me on the road. Jill wanted and needed me at home, but I threw myself into work. Her response was more distance and bitterness when I was home. We were on the ropes, big time. A lot of professional athlete marriages don't make it, probably for a variety of reasons— travel, other women, and unrealistic expectations—but add to that a terminally ill child, and we were on the ropes.

When I was home, it seemed like I couldn't do anything right. Jill had taken over in my absence because she had to. It was a necessity, and her strong character allowed her to do so. But when I came home, I just interrupted the flow of how everything ran without me.

Jill was growing to know our son in a deep way and bonding with him in ways that my words can't express. She slept with him at night because of his medical needs, meaning that she couldn't sleep with me. That was just one illustration of the distance in our relationship. I was a master at healing rifts in the locker room and talking to the media, but I couldn't reach out to my own wife when she needed me most.

For the first time in my life, really, I was failing. I was facing a challenge I couldn't conquer—both in terms of Hunter's disease and my growing distance from Jill. And for the first time, my response to failing was to stop trying.

Even though I didn't understand what praying was all about, I prayed all the time for a miraculous change in our circumstances...for Hunter to be healed. But what I really needed was a change in my heart. I needed a hope that couldn't be bought with all the money, fame, and resources on the planet.

For Jill and me, our religions (both of us being raised Catholic) were always about what *we* could do—how many times we went to confession and how many Hail Marys we could say. But what we really needed was something that only God could do for *us*, and it would ultimately save our family and change the course of our lives forever.

> *Dear Cam and Erin,*
>
> *You are two of the most responsible people I know, and I'm thankful for that! Life is about shouldering additional responsibility. Sometimes you have so much that you feel like you can't take any more, and that is when you'll need to rely on the Lord to get you through. There is something to be said for taking responsibility when we're wrong as well—admitting it publicly, if necessary, and apologizing. There's great freedom in being humble enough to do that.*
>
> *Love,*
> *Dad*

OFFENSIVE STRATEGIES

1. What are the most challenging responsibilities in your life?

2. Why is it so hard to admit when we're wrong?
3. How do you encourage your children to deal with life's responsibilities in a healthy way?
4. How are you gradually increasing their responsibilities as training for adult life?

Teamwork: What Is a Hero?

Dear Hunter,

    I thank God for your life. I thank God for the trials that our family walked through together. I thank you for the way that you taught us to live, each day, to the fullest. My life, today, is a flurry of activity—meetings, appearances, and radio interviews—but in all of it, I remember you, and I thank God for you. You're my hero, my soldier, and always my son.

Always,
Your dad

Faith is being sure of what we hope for, and certain of what we do not see.

                      —Hebrews 11:1

A friend loves at all times.

                      —Proverbs 17:17

I'm writing from my office, where I'm preparing for the annual NFL/Kelly family circus that is the Super Bowl. I've gone to the Super Bowl with my brothers for the past twenty-five years, I believe. The week is a crazy blur of interviews and appearances, hand shaking, back slapping, remembering names, pretending to remember names, autograph signings, and remote broadcast tables. There are lots of headsets. Lots of "happy to be heres." Then, at the end of the evening, starting around nine p.m. or so, I get to do what I came to do, which is hang out with my brothers.

The Super Bowl is awesome, but it's a celebration of everything shallow. I try to use it to raise awareness for our foundation and some other great organizations, but in reality it's a two-week orgy of money, fame, and all of the things that will never last. It's weird to be a part of it. But here's the thing: it's also about football, and when this week is all over, the thing I'll enjoy the most is the game. I'll enjoy the quarterbacks—this year it's Aaron Rodgers (Packers) and Big Ben Roethlisberger (Steelers), who has become a friend. I'll root for both of them because I like both of them. One thing I learned in four Super Bowls is that once all the interviews, hype, and craziness is over, it's just another game—a hundred-yard field with a defense to figure out.

I'm looking at an old copy of *Jim Kelly: Armed and Dangerous*, which is the book I wrote with Vic Carucci back in 1992. I'm on the cover in a Bills jacket with slicked-back hair (and, incidentally, no shirt on under my jacket, which begs the question, "What the heck was I thinking?"), looking like I was ready to take on the world. It was sort of your typical jock biography in that almost every story featured me doing something awesome and almost everything turned out my way. We ended that book with the sentence, "I can't predict the future, but I believe the best is yet to come."

In a way that was the most arrogant, shortsighted, and immature way to possibly end a book, but in an odd way it was also completely true. I would lose two more Super Bowls, retire, be inducted into the Pro Football Hall of Fame, and then be taken on the wild journey that is life with a special-needs child. That experience would change my life and ultimately save my marriage.

Retirement was tough. Even though I still had fame and acclaim because I was former Bills quarterback Jim Kelly, there's nothing like the identity that comes from playing football. And there's nothing that can compare to the actual *playing* of the game. Truth be told, everything else seems pretty boring by comparison. And the way I went out was tough too. Nobody can really choose how they want to go out, and by the end the Bills had brought in another quarterback they liked, and he was getting some opportunities to lead the offense that I had led all those years. I never said it then, but the reality of that killed me. It kills every old player. It's part of the life cycle of the professional athlete.

My last game was a playoff game in 1996 against the Jacksonville Jaguars in Rich Stadium. It was a balmy 48 degrees in Buffalo, which should have been our first indication that it would be an unusual Bills playoff game. Our cast of characters had already changed considerably. Thurman and Andre were still there, but defensively Darryl, Cornelius Bennett, and Shane Conlan were all gone, and we were playing with a mostly new cast in the secondary as well.

But Bruce Smith was still there, and he forced Jacksonville's young quarterback, Mark Brunell, into an intentional grounding call on his own one-yard line on their first drive. For proof that this game was an example of eras and generations colliding, Brunell still drew an NFL paycheck in 2010 as a backup for the New York Jets. He had an amazing season in 1996, leading the NFL in passing yards with more than 4,300 and adding almost 400 yards rushing.

I, on the other hand, had hamstring troubles and a horrible start to the 1996 season. I threw four picks and hurt my hamstring in a loss to the Steelers in Week 3 and in Week 4 had to see Todd Collins running my offense at Rich Stadium against the Cowboys, which was as surreal as anything I've experienced on a football field. For the first time since my redshirt freshman year at Miami, I wasn't a starting quarterback because I was injured. But by the playoff game, I was feeling better and playing better. At the time I was third all-time in NFL postseason passing yards, with more than 3,600. Thurman was playing on a sore ankle, and I still had Steve Tasker, who was getting more reps at wide receiver, and Andre Reed starting with me.

Because of the near-safety in our playoff game against the Jags, we had great field position, and on our very first offensive play I hit Quinn Early, who we had picked up as a free agent from New Orleans, on a deep dig for a first down. By 1996 Ted Marchibroda was long gone, and we weren't running nearly as much of our offense out of a shotgun as we had before. Everything just felt a little bit different. But Thurman was still Thurman, and on a third down out of the shotgun I hit him out of the backfield and he raced into the end zone for our first score, on a play that felt like it came right out of 1989 or 1990. I pumped my fists and pointed to heaven, where I knew my mother who had just passed away was watching me.

Thurman's TD was his nineteenth in the postseason, which at the time was the most in NFL history. That stat just spoke to our postseason experience as a team. We had thirty-five guys on our roster with postseason experience and a combined 333 playoff games played.

That would be the last touchdown pass of my NFL career.

Our defense, led by coordinator Wade Phillips, was number one in the NFL against the rush, and early on Jacksonville was having trouble moving the ball. We had picked up 340-pound defensive tackle Ted Washington and veteran defensive end Jim Jeffcoat, who had played for all those great Dallas Cowboys teams, and they were making it impossible for the Jaguars to get Natrone Means and their ground game started.

All year people had questioned my arm strength, but I think more than arm strength, I just needed time to set up and throw. I was taking more traditional drops that year than I had in my whole career. Often, even on third downs, I would be lined up under center, which just meant that each play needed a little bit longer to develop.

We went to the proverbial well one time too many in the first half, when deep in our own territory I threw another shovel pass that was intercepted for a touchdown by Jags defensive end Clyde Simmons. The shovel pass is meant to take advantage of a defensive line that flies upfield, but Simmons was a cagey vet, and he stayed home and intercepted the pass. He had his eyes on me the whole play and stopped his rush right in front of Thurman. But I treated that pick like any other I had thrown in my career, which is that as soon as it happened, it was over and I moved on. You can't dwell on those things.

We scored our only two touchdowns in the first quarter. At the end of another long drive, Thurman ran a countertrap to the right side and walked into the end zone untouched. Thurman waited patiently behind Ruben Brown and tight end Lonnie Johnson, demonstrating the kind of vision and feel that made him a Hall of Famer. By that point, toward the end of the first quarter, we had outgained the Jags 127 yards to 4.

Our opening drive in the second quarter was a good example of how drastically things had changed, offensively, in Buffalo. We came out in a double tights (two tight ends), two-back, I-formation, and ran off tackle the first play before running a dive to the fullback on the second play. I was always more comfortable spreading the field. This felt kind of foreign to me.

I was stopped on a quarterback sneak in the second quarter, when we came up short by about an eighth of an inch. That play provided a big momentum shift, and the Jaguars scored later on a 30-yard Natrone Means run. Our offense couldn't finish drives, and the best offense we could muster was a pair of Steve Christie field goals and a Jeff Burris interception return for a touchdown.

Ironically, I can't remember the last play of my career. I fumbled twice before being sacked and sustaining my last concussion (of many). Everything from that point on, for me, is a blur. You walk off the field in this kind of fog where you know that things are happening around you, but they're just happening slower—or it's like they're happening farther away.

A Mark Brunell to Jimmy Smith touchdown pass tied the score at 27, and a Mike Hollis field goal sealed it for Jacksonville. And just like that our season, and my career, was over.

Losing One Team, Gaining Another

I announced my retirement at a press conference in the Bills practice facility. Jill was nine months pregnant. I had to stop several times during the speech to keep from crying. "I've had to make the most difficult decision in my entire life. I've been playing the game of football for over twenty-eight years. Many of my dreams have been fulfilled, many goals have been achieved, but most important to me, I've been able to take care of the people I love. So today, I stand before you to officially announce my retirement from the Buffalo Bills and the National Football League. To leave and not be a part of this team is something that will be very difficult to swallow," I said, with my teammates like Thurman, Bruce, and Kent Hull looking on. "I also know, in my stomach and in my heart, it's time to move on. I don't want to go out the way some other quarterbacks went out. I want to go out with some dignity, with respect from my peers, respect from my teammates. I wanted to retire a Buffalo Bill."

I didn't want to be one of these quarterbacks that hung on forever. There were guys I really respected who did that—like Joe Namath who played for the Rams at the end of his career and Johnny Unitas who ended his career with the Chargers—but I really didn't want to drift around the league until I wasn't wanted anymore. Still, it was tough because my 1983 classmates Dan Marino and John Elway were still playing at a high level. At the end I said, "To me, my life is just beginning," because that's what you're supposed to say when you're retiring, but many players (myself included) struggle to actually mean it.

Bills owner Ralph Wilson said, "There's no player who has done so much for the Buffalo Bills as Jim Kelly."

I retired with more than 35,000 passing yards and 237 touchdowns. As an athlete, what you've done in your life is always reduced to numbers on a page. That's the other tough thing about retirement—those numbers will never change, and you always think about the touchdowns you *didn't* get. It's kind of like money in the sense that *enough* is really never enough. *Enough* is always *one more*.

When Jill was pregnant with Hunter, she knew we were having a boy, but she didn't tell me. She wanted to keep it a surprise, and I know that keeping it to herself was one of the hardest things she's ever done.

On Valentine's Day, also my birthday, my son Hunter came into the world.

Hunter James Kelly was born on February 14, 1997, just a couple of weeks after my retirement and on my thirty-seventh birthday. Jill had kept his gender a secret, and I was overjoyed that I had the son I'd always dreamed of. Coming from a family of six boys, some of whom had already had sons of their own, there was no shortage of pressure. Still, I was just elated. In the delivery room I kept shouting, "It's a boy! It's a boy!" over and over. He was seven pounds, fourteen ounces.

Naturally, I called Thurman Thomas, who is one of my closest friends, to rub it in because Thurman and Patti had three girls, and I wanted to rub it in a little. I called and left a message that said, "Did I tell you that I had a son, a boy, born on my birthday? Just in case you didn't hear me the first time, I had a boy, yes, a boy."

I was flying. I couldn't tell people fast enough. I didn't even mind telling the media, who had gathered at the hospital when they got wind of the newest Kelly. I was already writing his future story in my head—football hero, hunting companion, and best friend. Before I went out to talk to the media, Jill smiled at me and said, "Happy birthday." No kidding.

I had already planned everything out, the script was already written—he would wear number 12 and play quarterback, and my brother Danny's son Zac, who was born eleven days before Hunter, would wear number 83 and play wide receiver. I dreamed of all the football games, hunting trips, and fun we would have together. I had his life completely planned out.

We found out four months into Hunter's life that he had Krabbe disease, and I truly can't describe the feeling I had when we found out. I can't describe the pain. I wouldn't wish that feeling on my worst enemy. So many dreams died that day. And for the first year of his life we woke up each morning wondering if that day would be our last with Hunter. We were told he'd be dead before his second birthday. We were told to take him home, make him comfortable, and wait for the day when he would go to be with Jesus.

Krabbe disease, according to the doctors, is a rare, often fatal degenerative disorder that affects the myelin sheath of the nervous system. This condition is inherited in an autosomal recessive pattern (note: I had no idea what this meant, pre-Hunter) which is a way that a trait or disease can be passed down through a family. The disease is named for the Danish neurologist Knud Haraldsen Krabbe (see also: Names I never thought I'd have to learn). Infants with Krabbe disease are normal at birth, just like Hunter was. Symptoms begin between the ages of three and six months with irritability, fevers, limb stiffness, seizures, feeding difficulties, vomiting, and slowing of mental and motor development. In the first stages of the disease, doctors often mistake the symptoms for those of cerebral palsy. Other symptoms include muscle weakness, spasticity, deafness, optic atrophy and blindness, paralysis, and difficulty when swallowing. Prolonged weight loss may also occur. There are also juvenile- and adult-onset cases of Krabbe disease, which have similar symptoms but slower progression. Krabbe's occurs in roughly one out of every one-hundred thousand births.

I was mad at God for Hunter's disease. I was mad that it had to be me, after all the stuff I'd done for charities and foundations and the way that I'd always had a soft spot in my heart for Down syndrome kids. It sounds horrible to say it, but I think I was expecting God to "reward" me for all that I'd done for charities and disabled kids. That kind of mind-set is just one example of the kind of skewed theology and logic I was operating with at the time. I was operating under the misconception that if I did good things for people, God would reward me with an easy life. The fact is that He rewarded me with exactly the life He knew I needed. In retrospect, maybe God was preparing me with all of that to have Hunter. It's impossible to fully know the mind of God, so I'll never know. God was pushed on me early in my career by some of the Christian guys on my team, but I resisted. Back then, it seemed like God was just an excuse to judge other people and feel superior. I had no idea what He had in store for me and the blessings that I had coming, even through the fire that was to come.

Meanwhile, the experience was taking its toll on my career and on my marriage to Jill. I had just retired and was trying my hand at TV stuff—I did some color commentary on NFL games for NBC Sports in 1997, and I also tried doing studio work for ESPN, but to be honest my personal and home life were in such turmoil that I couldn't really concentrate on any of it. At home we had a severe lack of communication. I just knew that whatever I did with or for Hunter, it wasn't right. Daddy couldn't hold him right... and really couldn't do anything right.

Jill dealt with the disease like the type-A leader she was and still is. She did all of the reading and most of the communicating with doctors. She was like an athlete preparing for a game. She wanted to know exactly what she was dealing with and how to attack it. She was also amazing and intentional when it came to raising our daughters. Even though Hunter was the focal point of so much of our attention, Jill made sure she made the girls a priority too, setting aside one day each month where each child got her full attention and got to plan the entire day. And the kids were amazing together. Inexplicably—because it's hard to know the minds of children (and God, come to think of it)—Hunter would relax around his sisters. He would relax his body when they snuggled. His eyes would light up when they walked in the room.

And even though I was away a lot, I noticed how the girls responded to their brother. They loved him dearly in spite of his differences, and when they played, they even pretended that their dolls had Krabbe's. It was like it was hardwired into them to love and care for Hunter.

One of the things I love about Jill most is the fact that she's a general. She's a take-charge kind of person and is a lot like me in that regard. That's one of the reasons why we fell in love, initially, because we had mutual respect for each other. It's also one of the things that made this whole process so difficult.

Teamwork through Trial

We were in the emergency room four to five times per year with Hunter, each time wondering if it would be our last. The ambulance would rush off into the distance, with Jill and Hunter on board, and often I would stay home comforting the girls, who I know were terrified.

But somewhere along the way we decided to stop treating Hunter like he was dying and start treating him like he was living. We determined that we were going to enjoy each day that we had with him. We did turkey calls and elk calls together, and when the Bills were playing badly on Sundays, we would throw in tapes of Dad's old football games and watch them together. Watching football with my son was one of the things I dreamed about, and it was good to live that dream with Hunter. It was good to watch some of those games and be reminded that I was still the guy who did some of those things on screen.

It was a great deal of work just to care for him on a day-to-day basis. Jill was afraid to leave the house, and when she did leave, even for an hour, she worried about Hunter the whole time. Her life was a cycle of feeding, physical therapy, Albuterol, chest therapy, exercise, medication, Tylenol, massage, and Jacuzzi. It was a nonstop, daily cycle. Every page in her day planner, for all those years, reflects each of those responsibilities. Still, we adored him.

Only a family with a special-needs child can understand what that's like. Our house looked like a hospital, to a certain degree. There were all kinds of plastic bins full of medical equipment and all of the special apparatuses that Hunter needed. We had a feeding pump, oxygen tanks, wheelchairs, a stander, and this thing called a suction machine which cleared sputum out of Hunter's throat and was every bit as awful as it sounds. There were always medical people around. Our home was no longer our own, to a certain degree, and that was hard for me. I love people, but I've always valued my privacy too. We rarely ate dinner alone as a family.

It was a great deal of work just to give Hunter a few "normal" childhood experiences. We have video of him playing the piano...in which he was positioned in his chair behind a keyboard and we would move his arm up and down, pressing the same key. It's both inspiring and at times heartbreaking to see that. He would "paint" in much the same way. We would put a marker or a crayon in his hand, and he would move his arm forward, pressing it down on the canvas. Those accomplishments might seem tiny to the rest of the world, but they meant everything to us. We celebrated all of them. All the while, Jill was pleading to God for help and clinging to His promises just to get through each day and enjoy Hunter.

There was so much richness in those days that we decided to live to the fullest. We're forever indebted to the team of people around us who allowed us to enjoy and experience every moment with him. We put our trust in those people, and they will forever be a part of our lives and our memories of Hunter. And I can't help but feel that Hunter had a permanent impact on them as well.

Bonnie, his teacher, said, "Although Hunter was the student and I was the teacher, I feel like I left your home feeling like I was the student. Your son taught me so very much about life, about God, and about himself." Kristin, his speech therapist, said, "Not only did Hunter love to learn, he loved to teach. He taught everyone around him about courage, thoughtfulness, patience, and trust." Ellen, his nurse, said, "Faith, hope, and love, along with a willingness to learn, can change the world."

Hunter had a friend named Robert. Robert was a kid his age who would trade toys with Hunter through his mom, who was one of our physical therapists. Soon an amazing and real friendship developed. Robert was amazing in the way that he played with Hunter. Hunter had learned to communicate by blinking and holding his eyes wide open. Robert picked right up on that. Robert said, "We did all of the things kids do—we played, talked, watched movies, read books together, and had lots of fun. We built forts in his family room and shone flashlights on the ceiling. We played card games. I couldn't read Hunter's mind or anything, but he seemed to really have fun when we were together." He did, Robert. And you were a godsend. Robert introduced Hunter to all the boy stuff that he would have never experienced otherwise—rescue hero toys, Bionicle fights, and Silly String. It was amazing.

Even though he couldn't speak, Hunter had an innate ability to connect with people, and his personality was tangible proof of God's goodness. Even before I realized it, his life was drawing people nearer to the Lord. "From the first moment I looked into those big, beautiful green eyes, I knew I was in love," Tammy, his nurse, wrote. "Never before have I met a person so full of life in Christ. Knowing you and being blessed to be a part of your life the last eight years has made me a better person, restoring and renewing my faith in God. I don't know anyone who enjoyed life more than you." Barb, another nurse, would break out in praise songs when she was giving Hunter his treatments. She said, "I will always treasure the time I had with him and will look forward to the day when our voices will be raised together with the angels, singing praise to our Creator together."

And Kathy, Hunter's occupational therapist, may have said it best when she said, "It takes someone full of wisdom to change lives. God, in His wisdom, chose a child. He chose Hunter James Kelly. God is good."

There is so much truth in her words, and we are proof that God's plan is good and right, even if we don't understand it fully at the time. And at the time I didn't. I was angry, and I struggled mightily. I was supposed to be "enjoying life" because I had all of the trappings, supposedly, that came with an enjoyable life—money, toys, and a successful career to look back on. Except that my heart was in a constant posture of rebellion with God. God was trying to teach me a lesson through Hunter, but I wasn't ready to learn. I was the only one, it seems, who wasn't learning.

My miscommunication with Jill lasted literally until the

day Hunter died. I got a call from my father-in-law that Hunter had quit breathing and had to go to the hospital, and I assumed she took him to Children's Hospital because that was where we usually went. But it turns out Hunter was at another hospital (Warsaw), and I had gone to the wrong place. I sat in the emergency room at Children's for what seemed like forever before I checked with a nurse, and she said that I needed to go to Warsaw right away. I could tell by the way she said it that something was wrong. I was mad that I'd wasted the time at Children's Hospital.

As I was speeding around Buffalo, headed toward Warsaw, I spotted a cop with his lights on in the rearview mirror. "You've gotta be kidding me," I thought to myself as I pulled over. Incidentally, and this may be divulging too much, but I pride myself on avoiding cops and traffic tickets. I've been in Buffalo so long that I know where they sit, and I feel like I've gotten pretty efficient at avoiding them. The cop came to my window and said, "Mr. Kelly, thank God it's you. We got a call about your son, and I'm going to escort you to Warsaw Hospital. Follow me." He had been out driving the back roads and looking for me the whole time. I was scared, but I knew Hunter was tough and he'd pulled through time and time again. I couldn't let myself think he could die.

When I arrived, they said I needed to go inside NOW. I thought that was strange, but when I got inside I knew why. A couple of doctors met me at the door and said, "I'm sorry, Jim, your son just passed a few minutes ago." I rushed into the room where Jill had been for a long time and where she sat now with her head lying next to Hunter's body. I rushed to his side and said, "Hunter, Daddy's here now, little buddy. I'm here." Jill left the room because she couldn't bear to see me. My eyes filled with tears.

It's one of those things, of course, that people say they'll never forget. You never forget the way the hospital looks and smells on a day like that. The beeping stuff in the background. The people getting paged over the loudspeaker. The sense of injustice at the fact that my life as I know it has just ended/ changed forever, but lots of other peoples' lives are just going on like normal. There are doctors going home, nurses making plans for after work, and lives just grinding away. It seemed cruel that I wasn't able to say good-bye to Hunter. All of the money and fame didn't mean a thing in that moment. The fact that we had the best treatment and the best doctors because we lived in Buffalo. I sat in the offices of world-renowned doctors all over the world and looked at their impressive degrees on the walls and nodded at their huge semicomprehensible words. We did it all, and would do it all again, for just another day with him.

All of that—the doctors and the treatments—was all a part of "the fight" that we engaged in day after day as a team. And as soon as Hunter died, I felt a void. I missed him, of course, desperately. It's the kind of pain and grief that stays with you and puts you in a fog. It's like a postconcussion fog of grief. Everything is just a little duller, and life is a little slower for a while. And the pain in my heart was tangible every day. I didn't express it much. I was devastated that night. Devastated that he was gone, and devastated that I had to find out that way. I couldn't believe it. Jill and I didn't say a word on the drive home, which was a precursor to the way that we grieved—which was mostly separately.

I dealt with it by staying in motion, but there was the sense that life shouldn't go on because our lives had been so shattered.

Reminders of Hunter were all over the house. His clothes, his rescue heroes toys, and even the oxygen tanks that had become such a huge part of our lives. His Quickie wheelchair. The van we had made specially for him, that we only had for two months before he died. There was this therapy vest that he had, with stickers of superheroes and David and Goliath on it. There were US Army stickers on the machine too—my mother-in-law had given Hunter the nickname "Soldier Boy" because of his courage and bravery. Hunter received the 2003 Good Scout Award for Bravery, given by the Boy Scouts of America—Greater Niagara Frontier Council. There was an award ceremony that Robert and Hunter attended, dressed to the nines. Before the ceremony, Hunter wrote a speech with Jill, blinking at the things he wanted included so that the words were his:

> First of all, I just have to tell you that I'm feeling pretty important with this fancy shirt and tie on. I only dress up like this once a year for our family Christmas picture, so this is cool for me.
>
> This is such a great day! Thank you so much for honoring me this afternoon with the Boy Scout Award for Bravery. I did not know what it meant to be brave until now. For a six-year-old boy to stand up here in front of all of you—now that's brave.

When my mom and I talked about bravery the other day, a few thoughts came to my mind. To me, bravery is:

Like a tiny fish in a big blue sea or a birdie learning to fly

Being strong even when it hurts

Telling you how I feel deep in my heart

Watching kids run and play and telling them, "Great job"

Stretching my arms and moving my head all by myself

Catching my breath

I'm very happy to be Hunter James Kelly. Although I am unable to do a lot of things, I am able to do what is most important, and that is to love. God is so good to me. He blessed me with a very important mission here on earth, and all of you are helping me achieve it. Hunter's Hope is so special to my family and me. You all have been so generous in helping us to raise awareness and funds to help my friends with this terrible disease. And believe me, this disease is awful.

But more important than all of that, God asked me to teach all of you about Him and His amazing love for all of us. Sometimes we get carried away with the things of this world that really don't matter, when all that really matters is that we fulfill the purpose for which God created each one of us. My purpose is to show all of you that God's love is the best and that prayer really can move mountains and give strength to the weak and hope to those who have none.

You see, it's not about me, it's about Him. I love being a six-year-old boy, but I love being God's little warrior even more. I'm thankful for God and all the people that love me and help me be brave. Please keep me in your prayers, and thank you again for this very special honor.

My daughter Camryn was nine when she wrote a tribute to Hunter:

...I miss Hunter's warm, soft skin and his smile. I miss kissing his cute face every morning and touching his wavy hair...I loved my big brother so much and didn't want to let him go. I know that God had a plan for Hunter's life, and He has a plan for my life too...The most terrible moment in my life was when my mom, dad, and grammie told me that Hunter went to heaven. I cried my eyes out. I didn't want it to be true. But it was. We were all crying. I still cry sometimes...Hunter would always brighten up my day. I love my brother so much that sometimes I feel like my heart will explode. I wish he were still here with me, but I know that heaven is the best home for him and all of us...I can't wait to see Hunter again, and I can't wait to see Jesus.

My daughter Erin was thirteen when she wrote Hunter this letter. Erin is more like me. She has a hard time talking about all of this to other people. Much of her grieving is inward.

Dear Hunterboy,

No words can express how much I love you...You mean more to me than anything in the entire world. The best day of my life was when you came into my life, and the worst was when you left. I know I will see you again someday soon in eternity. But I would do anything to be with you for one more day...even if it was only for a second...Life will never be the same without you. Home isn't home without you. Life isn't life without you. I'll never be the same. Jesus is the only reason I'm still living...I know God had a reason for your suffering, even though I don't understand it all. You were put in my life for a reason. If it were not for God blessing me with you as my brother, I would be lost in this broken world. You are a breath of fresh air. When I look at you, I don't see "disabled"; I see my only brother—who is very able. Because you, Hunter James Kelly, are a life changer. You changed my life without a word, and because of you I will never be the same. I can't wait to spend eternity with you. You're the world's best brother. I love you more than life itself.

I can't believe how well the girls are able to express what's in their hearts and minds. It's an inspiration to me.

Honestly, it was more than hard. I would see fathers and sons, and it would remind me of what I'd lost. I wondered how a loving God could do that to Hunter and to our family.

And at the time I had no idea that those questions were leading me toward a truth and peace that surpassed my understanding.

On my forty-sixth birthday, and what would have been
Hunter's ninth, Jill and I drove out to the cemetery to see his
grave. I knew that Jill was hurting, but she tried her hardest to
make it a special birthday—decorating the house for Valentine's Day like we always had. When we got to the cemetery,
I decided I wanted to make a snowman for Hunter, so we used
black licorice for the eyes and mouth and put a Buffalo Bills
hat on his head.

I decided to give Jill a gift that year. My gift was that for a
half hour every week I would sit down, turn off the phone,
and let Jill teach me about Jesus and the Bible.

I don't think about the Hall of Fame too often, but there are
reminders all over my house. I have helmets in a trophy case
in my office at home that are signed by as many of the Hall of
Famers as I could get. Some of them I keep because deep down
in addition to being a football player, I'm still a fan. Most of
them I auction off to raise money for Hunter's Hope. The helmets are white with the Hall of Fame logo on the side and a
bunch of black signatures. I've got them in glass under lights.
The helmets sit next to AFC championship rings and my Wall
of Fame ring from Miami. I struggle with how much to show
it all off in the house. But the truth is, I like looking at it and
remembering and reminiscing about the days when I had so
much fun with my teammates and family. I'm proud of it, to
some degree.

I remember the induction ceremony and Marv Levy's
speech to introduce me. Marv said, "In an era of headsets and
burgeoning technology, he did it the old-fashioned way, call-

ing his own plays right up there at the line of scrimmage. What a swashbuckling figure he cut as he led our team on drive after drive into our opponents' end zone. If they were to make a movie about the life of John Wayne, Jim Kelly ought to play the part."

When I got to the podium, I said, "It is only fitting that I would follow Marv. For years people have always credited me with being the leader of the Bills. But I can honestly tell you that the real leader of our great team is that man right there, Marv Levy." And I meant every word of that. There are so many coaches out there, and to get one as classy, intelligent, and full of character as Marv Levy was a huge blessing. Marv used to say that he would only go after players with character to fill our roster—guys who didn't have reputations for getting in trouble or skipping practices. But I have to say that the character and resiliency we had on those teams started with Marv.

I remember how good it felt to be onstage in Canton with all the other guys in yellow sport coats and how it felt to be included with Dan Hampton, John Stallworth, George Allen (represented by his son), and Dave Casper in my class. During Hall of Fame induction week, there are all kinds of parties and receptions, and for a week this small town in Ohio is flooded with rabid football fans. There were huge banners with a picture of all of our faces on it that hung over the side of Fawcett Stadium—the same place where I had watched my brother play for the Lions all those years ago and dreamed about one day playing in an NFL uniform.

There is the unveiling of the "bust" (the head statue) that will forever be in the Hall of Fame. I have a replica of the bust in my hunting lodge. The bust never really looks exactly like you, but you don't care because you're in the Hall of Fame. It was both beyond any of my wildest dreams and at the same time somehow less spectacular than I dreamed it would be. It was validation, in a sense, for all the hard work and the semi-obsession that I had with this game and with competing on the highest level. But here's the interesting part: I see those helmets almost every day, but the fact of the matter is that I don't get the "buzz" every day. There's a law of diminishing returns at work. The fact is that my body still hurts, and sometimes I can barely get out of bed in the morning because of my back, shoulders, and neck. It's something that all the guys, not only in the Hall of Fame, but who played football period deal with.

When I walked onto the stage that day in Canton, the crowd of fifteen thousand was chanting "Kelly, Kelly, Kelly!" I was walked to the podium and embraced by Chris Berman, the ESPN sportscaster, who is a friend, always supported the Bills, and attended a few of my postgame parties back in Orchard Park. And it was amazing to be onstage with John Stallworth from the Steelers, whom I had watched growing up.

The best part about the Hall of Fame was the opportunity it gave me to honor my wife, my daughters Cam and Erin, and my son Hunter onstage, and all the people that helped me achieve this wonderful honor, in a way that will be captured forever. I said that my wife Jill is the backbone and spiritual rock of the Kelly household. Her faith and her unselfishness make her the kind of mother every father wants for their children. She is Mother of the Year every day of her life. I thanked

God that Hunter was with us long enough to be at the induction, and I called him my hero, my soldier, and my son. I said it with tears in my eyes.

As I walk by those helmets and I walk around my house in the morning—it occurs to me (again) that I couldn't do any of it without my team. My team, back then, was Hull, Wolford, Thurman, Andre, Bruce, Frank, Tasker, Marv, Ted Marchibroda, and all the guys I think about whenever I think about football. But my team now is so much more important.

Jill truly is my spiritual anchor and my partner in all things. I've spent my whole life leading, but there are so many ways that she leads me—she's a scholar, a reader, a writer, and a spiritual leader for our family. Jill is the one with a big stack of books next to her nightstand . . . She's always growing mentally. And I'm so glad that the Lord is giving us the communication that eluded us for so many years. And our church is a part of that team—a part of the reason that it's happening now. I'm not ashamed to say that we see a counselor there, and he's been absolutely instrumental in helping us understand each other and grow closer together.

It's February 14th, which is my birthday, Hunter's birthday, and of course, Valentine's Day. Every year there are so many emotions in play on February 14th. I'm not usually the kind of guy who really talks about his emotions, but it's hard to ignore. Every February 14th my organization throws a big party called Hunter's Day of Hope for Children. We have a bunch of those inflatable NFL Experience things set up, and it's just a chance for parents to come out with their kids and really celebrate being a family. We have free hot dogs, pizza, games, and I usually give a short talk about the importance of

family and the importance of parents making a real invest-
ment in the lives of their kids. If there's one thing raising
Hunter taught me, it's to never take a single day for granted.
We usually have more than five thousand people out for
Hunter's Day of Hope, and for us it's a great, tangible way to
remember him and honor him.

And we were so touched by the way he was remembered
and honored. We even got a note from President George W.
Bush, which read, "Hunter's courage and strength are an
inspiration. Please know that you are in our prayers. May you
be comforted by your faith and the love and support of your
family and friends."

Let me paint a picture for you: my life is usually kind of a nonstop revolving door of people and I usually love that because
I'm an extrovert. But tonight my house is empty, except for Jill
and the girls. Cam and Erin set the table, and we had a great
birthday dinner together. They made me my favorite meal,
and everybody pitched in. Even me. Sitting here, with the
remnants of dinner still on the table and my girls around me,
I am beyond blessed. There's no place I'd rather be than right
here, right now, with my team.

> *Dear Cam and Erin,*
>
> *Your tributes to your brother were beautiful, and
> there's nobody I'd rather have on my team than you. If you
> learned anything from my years with the Bills, I hope it's
> that life is a team effort. Very little of what we do happens
> in a vacuum—our decisions impact our teammates, and*

having the right teammates can make or break our experi-
ences. My hope and prayer for you is that you'll surround
yourself with quality teammates and that you would work
hard to help and honor the people who take care of you
in life.

Always,
Your dad

OFFENSIVE STRATEGIES

1. How are you honoring the "teammates" in your life?
2. Who are the most important teammates in your life?
3. Why didn't Jim's experiences leading his teammates translate into success leading his family early on?
4. Do your kids feel like a valuable part of your team? If not, how can you work to develop this?

Spiritual Life: A Hope and a Future

> "For I know the plans I have for you," declares
> the LORD, "plans to prosper you and not to
> harm you, plans to give you hope and a future."
> —Jeremiah 29:11

Dear Hunter,
*   I can't wait to see you again. I miss you so much,*
buddy.

Love Always,
Dad

You know what I love? My truck. If that seems like a strange way to start a chapter on spirituality, it's because it is, I guess. But my truck is a refuge for me. It's like a big, black office on wheels—it's where I do a great deal of talking, thinking, and game planning both in terms of business and my spiritual life. The truck is as you would expect, probably. It's the kind of truck they sell a lot of on Sunday afternoons during NFL telecasts. The kind of thing that could pull a bunch of anvils up the side of a mountain. An alpha-male type of truck.

The truck is an integral part of life at Hunter's Haven Lodge, which is a hunting lodge I maintain in some beautiful hills south of Buffalo. The lodge is a haven for me—I designed it myself with some help from my cousin Ed, and it's covered, nearly wooden-floor-to-wooden-ceiling, in things that my friends and I have harvested on hunting trips. To the casual observer it may just look like another building with a bunch of animal mounts in it, but to me each of those animals is a beautiful reminder of God's creation, as well as a reminder of the kinds of friendships and relationships He's blessed me with.

Today I'm preparing the lodge for Pittsburgh Steelers quarterback Ben Roethlisberger, who is a good friend of mine, because we're both Pennsylvania guys (me, born and raised, and he now as a Steeler). I thought he could use some time away and invited him to come snowmobiling with friends.

The lodge is situated on one hundred fifty acres and includes a fully stocked pond for fishing and lots of four-wheelers, trails, and space for hunting and snowmobiling. It's basically the ultimate hideout, if I do say so myself. It's hosted many a party and many a symposium for our Hunter's Hope Foundation.

And no discussion of spiritual things can begin or end without a few words on the foundation. Jill and I feel especially called to care for families and individuals who are dealing with Krabbe disease. Hunter's Hope Foundation was established to address the acute need for information and research with respect to Krabbe disease and related leukodystrophies. In addition, we strive to support and encourage those afflicted and their families as they struggle to endure, adjust, and cope with the demands of these fatal illnesses.

Accordingly, our mission is four-fold:

- To broaden public awareness of Krabbe disease and other leukodystrophies, thus increasing the probability of early detection and treatment.
- To gather and provide current, functional information and service linkages to families of children with leukodystrophies.
- To fund research efforts that will identify new treatments, therapies, and ultimately a cure for Krabbe disease and other leukodystrophies.
- To establish an alliance of hope that will nourish, affirm, and confront the urgent need for medical, financial, and emotional support of family members and those afflicted with leukodystrophies.

We want to inspire an appreciation of all children and express a thankful heart toward God for these precious gifts of life. These bedrock values are categorically and vigilantly expressed throughout all of the foundation's programs and activities. First and foremost is funding for Krabbe disease research. There are approximately two million people in the United States who are carriers of the genetic defect that causes this disease. We also have furnished apartments available in Durham, North Carolina, for families with children hospitalized at Duke Hospital, and an equipment exchange to help families with their adaptive equipment needs. We also fund "Wish Gifts," which are grants to families with needs (like vans or other special equipment) that they previously thought unattainable. Finally, we're advocates for Universal Newborn Screening, which is a state-based, public health system that is essential for preventing the devastating consequences of all kinds of diseases. Because the level of screening varies from state to state, there are many newborns who are not being screened for rare diseases. For more information on all of these programs, visit www.huntershope.org.

The best part about the foundation, though, is the contact it gives us with other families around the country who are in the midst of their struggles with Krabbe's. It's really humbling each time we meet a child . . . and each time we're reminded of how God is using Hunter's life to touch others. We have an event each year called the Hunter's Hope Family and Medical Symposium, and it's a chance for us to be with families who are walking through this disease, just like we did.

I can't say enough about how amazing, courageous, and authentic these families are. Usually when you meet someone, it's because of a choice you've made. For example, I've been around football people my whole life because I'm a football player. But the foundation, and this disease, has given us the opportunity to meet these amazing families. They need encouragement, and we need their encouragement. The unconditional love they have for these kids is extraordinary. The joy they display as we celebrate their kids' accomplishments and progress is one of the most genuine things I've ever seen. I thank God for all of it. And I thank God for the progress that's been made. As I write this, there is a cord-blood transplant treatment available that can provide hope and healing for some of these children. I can't help but feel like some of that hope came from Hunter's suffering.

The foundation is sort of the outward manifestation of our spiritual lives, but the fact of the matter is that God has taken us on a pretty wild and unique journey. And even in the days when things seemed the most hopeless, He was there, working on our hearts to give us hope and a future.

The thing is, we were never "hopeless" in the sense of not having enough money or worrying about our futures in that sense. Ours was a very different feeling from the feeling my dad had growing up. He went through layoffs and lean years and the struggle of raising all those boys on not very much money. I'm sure it felt hopeless to him at times. For me, as soon as I signed my first USFL contract and then my subsequent NFL deals, I always had "enough."

Our crisis of hope came with Hunter—especially when Hunter died and our marriage was just barely hanging on and we were in the midst of a serious grieving process. I was angry at God. I didn't know how anybody could love a God who would allow, and even ordain, that much pain. But before I can finish that thought, spiritually, I have to go back to the beginning.

Growing up, everybody in our family, and nearly everybody in our town, was Catholic. Sit. Kneel. Stand. As kids we never really went into it to learn a lot, but we just went to go through the motions and please our folks. It was important to them, and we weren't ever allowed to miss mass. Now here's the thing: I could do the "typical" athlete thing and talk about how much I prayed and how God answered my prayer by allowing me to live my dreams and be a pro football player. And in a way that would be true. But the fact of the matter is, that had a lot more to do with God giving me some vocational gifts (throwing the football, being big, taking abuse), and I worked hard to develop them. And in a way, that would bum out all the other people who prayed just as fervently that God would allow them to do something like play pro football, only to see their dreams die. I don't know why God allowed me to play for the Bills and live some dreams. I certainly didn't deserve it any more than anyone else.

The fact of the matter is, the important part of the spiritual story is Christ's role in forgiving my sins. But again, I'm getting ahead of myself.

My brothers and I were all altar boys. And the attire they had us wear was too small for all of us because we were all big guys. We would always try to get to church early to get a seat in the back because nobody could see over us. When I got to be in tenth or eleventh grade, I talked my parents into letting me be a "commentator" at church, which meant that I got to do the readings. In my teenage logic, I preferred to be a commentator because I thought it looked more "professional" and "grown up." Whatever. By the time I was that age I had sat through so many masses that I could almost recite the homilies verbatim.

I always kind of had a weird relationship with the whole idea of the Christian athlete. When I came into the league all those years ago, it seemed like Christians were guys who looked down on you and silently (or not so silently) judged you. Back then, the idea of the Christian athlete as a "marketing tool" was just starting to kick in. You started to see entire magazines devoted to Christian athletes, and guys really started playing it up. So I distanced myself from it. I'm a firm believer in the idea that it's not necessarily what you say, but how you say it that means the most. You never want to push anything on anybody, in my opinion. With me it's always been about the question of, "How do I get them to believe in what I'm doing or thinking?" It's been this way in football, in business, with the foundation, and in any other aspect of leadership. The only Christian athlete I really admired at the time was my friend Frank Reich, who never pushed or forced anything on me.

The fact of the matter is, the Christian athlete landscape has changed since I played. You see a lot more guys praying at the center of the field after games than you did when I played. Now, that could be a function of a lot of different things— namely the fact that we play a dangerous game that could take our health and even our lives—but it's still good.

I didn't know how much I really needed my faith until Hunter died. I didn't know how to pray, and I didn't know where to look for answers. I wasn't that impressed with Christians, honestly. They seemed like Bible-thumpers who didn't know how to have a good time.

But I knew in my heart that if I wanted to see Hunter again in heaven, or if I wanted to walk in the front door of my house and see my daughters look at me with respect, I had to change. I knew if I continued that lifestyle I wouldn't be able to see my son again.

Now, that can sound a little shortsighted, like my whole motivation for trusting the Lord with my life was seeing Hunter. And initially that was part of it. I believe the Lord used that motivation to draw me near to Himself. I was interested in learning about heaven because to me heaven was where I could see my boy again. Jill was reading a book called *Heaven* by Randy Alcorn, and I was interested in what it said about the idea of a "resurrection body." Alcorn writes:

A fundamental article of the Christian faith is that the resurrected Christ now dwells in heaven. We are told that his resurrected body on Earth was physical, and that this same, physical Jesus ascended to Heaven, from which he will one day return to Earth (Acts 1:11). It seems indisputable, then, to say that there is at least one physical body in the present Heaven. If Christ's body in the intermediate Heaven has physical properties, it would stand to reason that others in Heaven might have physical forms as well, even if only temporary ones.

But most of all, I just wanted to feel some *freedom*. I was living a double life where I was trying to be the Community Leader and Family Man, but inside I knew my heart was sick. I wanted my daughters to be able to respect their father.

During our struggles with Hunter, Jill's uncle Mark had begun talking with her about the gospel. Really, he had just started answering the hard questions we both wanted answers to, but that only Jill was asking. Where is God in any of this? Why does God allow suffering? And why Hunter?

A Life, and a Faith, Changed

One of the important things about those talks was the fact that Mark had already been through some deep waters in his own life and was able to convey that to Jill. It's hard to sit and listen to someone who has never been through anything challenging talk about God's goodness. He didn't try to come up with pat answers to anything. He just shared the details of the gospel story—our sinful nature, our need for a savior, and God's love as illustrated through the birth, death, and resurrection of Jesus.

This was pretty mind-blowing stuff for a couple of Catholics who had been conditioned to think that "goodness" meant just showing up to mass and feeling guilty enough about stuff to go to confession.

Mark talked with Jill about an Old Testament character named Job, who suffered more than anyone in Scripture, lost all his wealth, and lost all ten of his children. I think what was most powerful to Jill, though, was the fact that Mark was different. He seemed to have a real sense of joy about him that's hard to describe.

When Jill became a Christian, I was convinced that I didn't want any of it pushed on me. I had heard and seen enough in the locker room. When I played ball, I felt like I didn't have time for any of it, and after football I was just mad at God because of Hunter. There were many times alone in hotel rooms on the road that I would just tear up a little and ask, "Why?"

Jill was grieving too and was struggling in her faith. She would spend hours some days curled up in a ball on the floor of her closet, just crying and reading her Bible. I know that there were days she didn't want to live. She wrote this in her journal: "I'm going to die if You leave me here. My life is but a breath, but this is not life to me. I can't drink this cup of suffering. I can't bear the weight of this cross. I can't live like this. Come quickly, Lord, and save me. I have no one but You, and yet You seem so distant. Have I allowed a mantle of doubt to hide me from the truth? I'm crushed in spirit. Search my heart. Save me. I have nothing if I don't have You."

She was clinging to the last shreds of hope, and she was beaten, but not ultimately destroyed. She never lost her faith.

And for the first time in my spiritual life, I was trying. The girls and I memorized Psalm 23 for Jill for Mother's Day one year. I agreed to see a marriage counselor from our church, which was (and still is) a huge part of my growth.

What's ironic is that I spent all that time in church as a kid but I didn't *know* anything about God. I never read the Bible, and I really didn't know anything about the God revealed in Scripture. And again, it's not all about knowledge. But if you say you love something, it makes sense that you have to know it. I love Jill. I can tell you what color her eyes are, and I can tell you her favorite foods, her favorite movies, and her favorite things to do. I love football and can tell you a million things about it. But I didn't know anything about God.

Until I became a Christian I never knew about the Old Testament. When I became a Christian and actually started reading the Bible, I started thinking, "Wow, this is exciting!" That's not to say I understand everything. I don't. But that's where the local church comes in. I get good teaching there, and I can ask questions of people who know more than me. I've never been the kind of guy who will drive around for hours, lost, in the truck. If I need directions, I'll stop and ask. I realized I needed spiritual direction.

A Desire for Freedom

Before I became a Christian, I was struggling with some fundamental questions. It sounds kind of shallow (in light of Hunter), but I wondered why the Lord would pick me to be the quarterback who was famous for losing four straight Super Bowls. I wondered why He would take Hunter, especially after I had done so many charitable things. It sounds horrible to give voice to that sentence, but it's true and honest. These are the kinds of things we ask ourselves in the quiet moments. And for a while I structured my life such—with television gigs and appearances—that there were no quiet moments. But I couldn't run forever.

I accepted Christ on April 23, 2007. It took me a while to get a full grasp, but I'm able to learn more, and I continue to be a work in progress. I'm a much better person today than I was five years ago. It's night and day. I'm a different, changed person. My fuse, temper-wise, is a lot longer. These are some of the fruits of the Holy Spirit... being slow to speak and slow to anger.

Jill wrote this in her journal in 2004, and I think it sums it up well: "Of all the gifts I'm most thankful for in this very moment, Lord Jesus, You're it. In this world with all its abundance, You are life to me. You are everything. You keep giving; there is no end to Your grace and goodness. In You I am held together. Held together with a love that binds parts of me that cannot function alone. If I rely on my brain, it will confuse me. If I rely on my body, I will fall apart. If I rely on other people, they will never meet my expectations. If I rely on my heart, it will bleed and break. When I look to You, Lord, and rely on You, I am whole and I can live."

I had spent my whole life relying on my body, my brain, and my resources. Those were good things—gifts from God—but they ultimately weren't enough. Jill, Jill's parents Jerry and Jacque, and Pastor Rich from our church helped me to see that only Christ could give me the freedom that I longed for. And only Christ could save my family.

I can't even describe the freedom of being *forgiven* for the things I'd done. I never knew what that felt like. It feels so much better. I knew that Christ and His death on the cross and resurrection was the only way for me to have my sins forgiven and was the only thing that would allow me to spend eternity in heaven and see Hunter again. It wasn't about how many Hail Marys I said, or how many times I went to church, or even how many thousands of dollars I gave to charitable causes. I couldn't earn my way into heaven. I just had to accept the free gift that Christ was giving me.

After Hunter was diagnosed and we started the foundation, it was hard work. It was hard to be around "it" all the time—"it" being the disease. I think my natural inclination would have been to just run away from it all. But we started meeting with these families, these parents whose kids have Krabbe disease. They would come up to us and say things like, "We were able to enjoy our son because of you guys." I can't tell you how good that felt. It gave a purpose to the suffering. Suffering is still suffering, and grief is still grief. There's not a day that goes by that I don't grieve for Hunter. Grief isn't a linear thing—meaning that you don't start at the beginning one day and then at some point in the future you're at the end. It circles around, and it keeps circling, but God continues to give us the grace to deal with it.

But because of Hunter we now know the Father's love through His one and only Son. And it's because of what God brought us through, with Hunter, that we can now be called children of God. I'm amazed by that. I'm amazed by how much, and how perfectly, God loved our family. Our hearts cry out because we miss him so much. But with every tear comes great hope because we know that one day we'll see him again. And until that day, we rest in God's perfect timing and plan.

My daughter Erin wrote, "Hunter is the most special boy in the world to me. He brightens up my day when I say 'hi' to him. I love saying verses with him and praying together. I love how he would always remind me to be strong and trust in God. I thank God for giving me the best boy, the toughest boy, my best friend, my brother Hunter. I love him very much!"

Wow. I can't read that without tearing up a little bit. I know that Jill wrote her book, in part, as a chronicle of what we went through and what God did for us and our family through Hunter. Because it's easy to forget. It's our nature, as human beings, to move on to the "next thing." This is the nature of football. There's always a new season and something new to be conquered. But these books are a way to tangibly remember and a way for our daughters (who were ten and six) to remember Hunter and remember God's love for us, even as life goes on. Even through the dramas of their life—the tests, the basketball games, the relationship troubles, and everything else. We want our daughters to be able to share this with their children and their grandchildren. They need to know that their mom and dad aren't perfect. Far from it. Our daughters need to know that they'll face trials in life, but that there is joy and peace in Christ.

I talk a lot more to Jesus now. I talk to Him in the tree stand when I'm hunting. I ask Him questions about life, I thank Him for things, and I ask Him for things. I still don't consider myself good at "praying." Sometimes when I'm praying, especially out loud, it feels awkward. But I'm good at talking, and one of my favorite things to do is talk to God.

On September 19, 2008, Jill and I renewed our vows at Hunter's Haven Lodge. Though we had been married in a church before, neither of us realized the depth of the commitment we'd made before God. We wanted to publicly acknowledge how God rescued us and our family.

Our daughter Erin asked if she could say a few words at the ceremony. She said, "Today you are standing in front of your friends and family, showing them that you are renewing your wedding vows because you are both now children of the Lord. You are showing your peers that, even now, after all you have been through, God is love and He is in control. And the verse I chose for you today is 1 Corinthians 13:4–8, 13: 'Love is patient, love is kind. It does not envy, it does not boast, it is not proud. It is not rude, it is not self-seeking, it is not easily angered, it keeps no record of wrongs. Love does not delight in evil but rejoices with the truth. It always protects, always trusts, always hopes, always perseveres. Love never fails... And now these three remain: faith, hope, and love. But the greatest of these is love.' "

I couldn't have said it better myself. Really, I couldn't. When I think of where God has brought us in the last ten years... it's indescribable. We don't grieve like those who have no hope. I love Jill and my daughters like I was never able to love them before.

I can't predict the future, but I believe the best is yet to come. And I mean it this time.

Dear Cam and Erin,

I am so thankful for your deep faith in our Lord Jesus Christ. It is that faith that allows me to fail, knowing that I have a redeemer who paid for my sins with His blood. This knowledge frees me to be a better father to you and a better husband to your mom. I'm thankful for what we've gone through because it has strengthened our faith. We know God in a way now that would have never been possible before. My prayer is that your faith will grow strong and that you'll grow nearer to the Lord as you grow up. Thank you for loving God and loving me.

Always,
Your dad

OFFENSIVE STRATEGIES

1. How did Christ change Jim's life?
2. Why didn't money, fame, and respect give Jim the peace in life that he longed for?
3. How does a desire for the respect of your children shape your thoughts and actions?
4. How are you tangibly, actively remembering the ways that God has taken care of you?
5. How are you encouraging your kids to grow in their faith?

Postgame Wrap-up

Dear Fathers,

I hope you enjoyed this collection of stories and encouragement, written both from my past as an athlete and from my present perspective as a father. Much of the "teaching" was done through stories—from things you may remember from my career with the Bills and things that have happened since. And while none of it is what I would call "groundbreaking" or "earth-shattering," there are principles—like humility, hard work, perseverance, and teamwork—that are timeless and that I hope will *always* be timeless. It seems like many of these principles are fading away in our society, and I think it's our job as fathers to preserve them and pass them along to our children.

If there's one thing I've learned through all of this, it's that being a father is hard work. It's hard work just like being a quarterback was hard, relentless work. It's often thankless work. But I can honestly say that it's the greatest, most important job in the world, and even quarterbacking in the NFL— which I counted an honor and a privilege—takes a distant backseat to raising my girls and the years that I spent with Hunter.

Football presented a great opportunity to see human beings reacting under pressure. It often brought out in great detail the fundamental elements of a man's character. It's amazing the things we're capable of—both good and bad—when we're under duress. In football it required playing hurt, dealing with difficult people, and taking a lot of scrutiny from others. It occurs to me that being a dad is similar. Fatherhood highlights our strengths and our weaknesses in profound ways.

Just know that as a father I've been down the road you're on now, and I'm right there with you, which is why I wrote this book. So enjoy the football stories, and challenge yourself to implement some of the principles. Work hard, pray for your children often, love your wives, and know that the job you're doing now, as a father, is the most important work you'll ever do!

All the Best,
Jim Kelly

Acknowledgments

Ted Kluck

It's pretty standard for professional writers to maintain some kind of journalistic distance when they write about someone. That was completely impossible with this project because as I wrote, I had pictures of my two sons, Tristan (8) and Maxim (5), on my desk and looked at them often. This is a book about fathers and sons. It's a book about husbands and wives. It's a book about loss, and it's a book about redemption. After writing it, I feel like I knew Hunter, and though I hesitate to write this for fear of what Jim might think, I cried when I wrote the section about Hunter's death. Actually I bawled my eyes out. There it is.

Thank you, Jim and Jill, for the privilege of being a part of this project. It was different from anything I've ever written, and it was challenging at times, but it was a blessing to me and to my family. I know God better, and I love Him more, because of it.

I'm thankful for my wife—for her patience, her kindness, her beauty, and her unconditional love for me. I'm thankful that she knows, loves, and serves the Lord. I'm thankful that in the personal valleys of our lives—the beatings we've taken—she's stood by my side, faithfully. Thank you for bearing with me through years of football and the several times I've broken my promises of being done playing. It's a hard habit to break.

We're imperfect people, living in a fallen world. My hope and prayer is that God would use us—imperfect as we are—through this book.

Thanks as always to my agent, Andrew Wolgemuth, for your friendship, for shepherding me through projects, and for securing new ones.

Jim Kelly

Well, like football, a book like this takes a team. And I would say that God has once again blessed me with an incredible team. Team Wolgemuth (Robert, Andrew, and Eric), Faith-Words (Joey Paul), Team Kluck (Yes, Ted—you're the man, but I know well that behind every successful man, there's a great woman. It's been a privilege to share my story and life with you. Bring your boys up for camp anytime. I'd consider it an honor to continue to pour what I have learned into their lives).

My wife, Jill—thank you...for...standing firm, loving the unlovely, forgiving every time, and loving Jesus for all to see. I've said this at least a million times—you're Mother of the Year every day of your life. Our children are blessed through you.

My daughters Erin and Camryn—Daddy loves you so much. This book is for fathers and sons, but I thought of both of you as we wrote. You make me so proud! Not a day goes by that I don't thank God for blessing me with two amazing girls. Thank you for loving me.

Hunterboy—no words can describe how much I miss you, love you, and wish that you were here with me. The heartbreak continues, but I know that we will be together—forever. Thank you for showing me what real courage is. Your life continues to change mine. And I hope that through this book God will continue to be glorified through His Son—because He showed me what life is all about through my one and only son. See you soon, little buddy!